SILENT SABOTAGE

SILENT SABOTAGE

Rescuing Our Careers, Our
Companies, and Our Lives
From the Creeping Paralysis
of Anger and Bitterness

WILLIAM J. MORIN

amacom

American Management Association

New York • Atlanta • Boston • Chicago • Kansas City • San Francisco • Washington, D.C.
Brussels • Mexico City • Tokyo • Toronto

Library of Congress Catalogining-in-Publication Data

Morin, William J.
    Silent sabotage : rescuing our careers, our companies, and
our lives from the creeping paralysis of anger and bitterness /
William J. Morin.
        p.   cm.
    Includes index.
    ISBN 0-8144-0300-X
    1. Social responsibility of business—United States.
2. Business ethics—United States.   3. Social values—
United States.   4. Corporate culture—United States.
5. United States—Moral conditions.   I. Title.
HD60.M67   1995
658.4'08—dc20   95-5618
                                                      CIP

Printing number

10   9   8   7   6   5   4   3   2   1

To my sons, Mark, Timothy and Jason, who daily make me glad the future is in the hands of people like them.

To my sister Martha and brother Earl, who have through the years been not only close loved ones, but also close friends.

To those men and women Teddy Roosevelt spoke about many years ago:

> "It is not the critic who counts, not the man who points out how the strong man stumbles, or where the doer of deeds could have done better. The credit belongs to the man who is actually in the arena, whose face is marred by its dust and sweat and blood; who strives valiantly, who errs, and comes short again and again . . .; who knows the great enthusiasms, the great devotions; who spends himself in a worthy cause; who at best knows in the end the triumph of high achievement; and who at the worst, if he fails, at least fails while daring greatly, so that his place shall never be with those cold and timid souls who know neither victory or defeat."
>
> —Theodore Roosevelt
> From his address at the Sorbonne,
> April 23, 1910

This book is dedicated to those human beings who try and try again.

Contents

Introduction   Read This—Most People Don't   1

Chapter 1   America's Values Crisis   9

Chapter 2   Why Value Values?   25

Chapter 3   What Happens When We Don't Care?   37

Chapter 4   What Motivates Us and What Must
Change?   51

Chapter 5   How to Rebuild Values in Your
Organization

   Step 1 in the Rebuilding Process   69

Chapter 6   Seeing Success for What it Really Is

   Step 2 in the Rebuilding Process   81

Chapter 7   Making It Work in Your Life and Your Company

Step 3 The Rebuilding Process   91

Chapter 8   A Call for Values   147

Appendix   What is *Your* Trust Level?   157

Glossary of Terms   167

Index   171

Acknowledgments

It is always a challenge to express appreciation and recognition to those persons, places or events that assisted in putting a book into print. Always, in the back of your mind, you are terrified you will miss someone or fail to say the right thing.

In any case, here we go with my best effort. First and foremost, I must recognize Mark Misercola who was the person who pulled all of my efforts together. His writing skills are too numerous to mention, and on top of everything, he is an excellent person. My able assistant and dear friend, Donna Wilson, is a very unsung hero on this whole project. Also our DBM publishing group of Al Longden, Jo-Anne Hand, Marina Boiadjian, Michele Ashley, and Andrew Hoffer all played major parts. The professional team at AMACOM were very helpful getting the book from a rough testament into a finished book. Finally, I must always mention the wonderful people at Drake Beam Morin from whom I draw my daily inspiration.

More praise for *Silent Sabotage*

"'Business is the business of America', so the accepted adage goes. Simple and true. Bill Morin's *Silent Sabotage* posits a more complex truth by fostering the possibility and necessity for equating the business endeavor with the best that is American. He stands squarely for a vision and virtue grounded in moral integrity."

—Emory N. Jackson
President
We Care About New York, Inc.

"*Silent Sabotage* includes excellent exercises in values identification and positive examples to stimulate leaders of educational and governmental institutions, as well as officers of both small businesses and large corporations, to develop ethics codes from within."

—Clark Davis
Professor Emeritus
Southern Illinois University

"Morin's position at DBM gives him a perspective on the values issue in corporate America that very few can match. He delivers the prescription of how to get well from a vantage point of someone who has taken the treatment himself. Very powerful!"

—James R. Emshoff
Chairman and Chief Executive Officer
IndeCap Enterprises, Inc.

"Bill Morin's *Silent Sabotage* should be read and then digested by all levels of management, and those institutions and groups who teach and advise business enterprises. Furthermore, if a top executive and, in particular, a chief executive is not leading with these principles, they should study them for applciation in their corporations."

—Donald J. Bainton
Chief Executive Officer
Continental Can Company, Inc.

Introduction

Read This— Most People Don't

"Many persons have a wrong idea of what constitutes true happiness. It is not attained through self-gratification but through fidelity to a worthy purpose."

HELEN KELLER

If, twenty years ago, a screenwriter had set out to write a dark, foreboding movie about life in the 1990s, it would be hard to imagine a more ominous scenario than the following:

- The world is gripped by scandal and instability. In Europe and Japan, governments routinely fall because of corruption, payoffs, and bribery. Government institutions are perceived as ineffective. In the United States, a majority of Americans say they do not trust their political leaders and question their ability to govern. They certainly do not see them as role models for themselves or their children. In the countries and states that once comprised the Soviet Union, military coups and open rebellions are common. Economically, many of these same countries are in serious trouble. In some Latin American countries, drugs and drug lords provide the only form of government. Urban areas are riddled by gang violence and drive-by shootings. Around the world, business is immersed in the whirlwind effects of "globalization," an all encompassing buzzword, which, for those unfortunate enough to be caught in the line of fire, has become synonymous with downsizings, layoffs, and accompanying separation trauma. It's not a pretty picture for the survivors either. For many, globalization means more work, greater stress, and less respect for the individual employee. Worker morale has collapsed. Profits and productivity go up and down so rapidly that no one can really tell who is winning or losing. In Australia, one out of every four jobs has been abolished. In the former Eastern bloc countries, millions have lost their once secure livelihoods. In the United States and Great Britain, the world's great defenders of freedom, people seek solace and escape from their worries in an ongoing circus of celebrity scandals—O. J. Simpson, Michael Jackson, the Royal Family, Tonya Harding, Lorena Bobbitt, Madonna—the list goes on. People everywhere are questioning their faith in any person or institution. Even the simple pleasures of American life, like baseball and hockey, have fallen victims to greed and stupidity. Everywhere, people are looking for answers. But instead, they find more questions.

You won't find such a movie in any theater or in your local video store. That's because this isn't a movie script. It's the here and now. It's real life. It's hard to believe that the reality of life could be worse than a science fiction film, particularly in light of the fact that the two great threats of the last half of the century—nuclear war and Communist domination of the world—have largely subsided. But it is. Instead of elation and optimism, we feel isolation and despair. We're fed up and frustrated. We've become a society of victims trying to figure out who to blame. We mistrust almost everyone. We see challenges as obstacles rather than as opportunities. This is how *Newsweek* described it during a recent election campaign: "Voters seem more melancholy and equivocal than outraged. They disdain all leaders and institutions in near-equal measure—the President, the Congress, the corporations, the media. Like Hamlet, they fret, but aren't eager for a world they know not of."[1]

[1] *Newsweek,* Nov. 7, 1994. "Rolling Thunder," page 24.

Yet, there are some parts of real life that we can't seem to get enough of. We seem to be obsessed with minutiae and gossip—who did what to whom and when. Both companies and individuals seem motivated by greed and envy. We treat people more like objects than human beings. We put "me" before "us" and "them." We value money and success above relationships and experience. And we blame the schools, the economy, our kids, and everybody else for our mistrust, frustration, and bitterness.

Chaos and unrest seem to be the rule rather than the exception. I once asked a colleague who happens to be a film buff about the future and he said, "Everyday, it's looking more and more like *Planet of the Apes,* and less like *Star Trek*."

What gives here? Is society as we know it coming apart at the seams? The headlines and talk shows certainly make it appear that way. I believe the problem goes much deeper than that. Neither our government nor our other institutions themselves are causing a crisis of confidence in society today. You and I are!

The crises of the Cold War have been replaced by a crisis of a different kind—a much more insidious and deeply rooted crisis: a *values crisis.* We are becoming a people without rudders, real values, and vision. The values we do cling to often have very little value at all. This, in turn, has given birth to a new phenomenon, a rarely examined social disease I call, "Silent Sabotage" that is tearing each of us and the very fabric of our society apart from within. What is Silent Sabotage? It's not one single problem, but the sum total of many problems converging at the same time. It's a turned-off, disenfranchised society that gives up in silent disapproval; it's a worker who comes in later and goes home earlier than he or she did ten years ago; it's a voter who gives up voting; it's people at work, at home, behind the wheel, anyplace at all—who just don't care enough about anything anymore.

Silent Sabotage manifests itself in different ways. It has virtually paralyzed government's ability to act as an agent of change. It has given us the great election paradox of our time; the public screams "down with incumbents, it's time for a change," but its new politicians don't seem to change compared with its old. We see it in our schools, which continue to turn out students who are ill-prepared to cope with the demands of the 21st century.

How bad is this Silent Sabotage? So bad that *Fortune* magazine recently reported that trust levels between students and teachers, employees and supervisors, and labor and management are at all-time lows.[2] It's so bad that when *Newsweek* asked its readers, "How much do you blame the following for the problems that make you dissatisfied?" a full 80 percent of the respondents listed the "moral decline of people in general" as the top problem.[3] Next in line was the news media. Unfortunately, no one bothered to ask the obvious question: What do we do about it?

The problems caused by Silent Sabotage are so deep and so pervasive that I'm not sure anyone fully understands its scope or where to look for a solution. One thing is certain—if we don't do something about it I fear that the result will be much like what best-selling author Michael Crichton writes: "The earth will continue to exist, but we as a species will not. Mother Nature has a way of disposing of things that are not

[2] *Fortune*, "State Your Value, Hold the Hot Air." April 1993, pp. 117–124.
[3] *Newsweek*, Nov. 7, 1994. "Rolling Thunder," page 31.

contributing, or contributing in the wrong way. The dinosaurs couldn't adapt to changing conditions around them. Likewise, we're not adapting when we need to. We're floundering. And we need to take account of what got us where we are; where we stand today, where we need to be going, and how we intend to get there."[4]

I believe there is only one way to overcome the effects of *Silent Sabotage*—by critically analyzing and re-evaluating our own values and our codes of ethics. And then rebuilding or reengineering them entirely. And because business has so much riding on the outcome, I believe industry has a special interest and role in the success of this endeavor. This book outlines a process that enables us to critically analyze and re-evaluate what is most important to each of us. It is designed to make us all think about where we are and where we're going. It is intended to help us recognize the symptoms of anemic values. It will refocus our priorities, and put us back on a track that will restore the balance that is so sorely missing from our lives.

At times, the process may ask too many questions and frustrate you with too few answers. This is not intentional. However, reengineering our values is still so new and uncharted that I don't claim to have all of the answers. The truth of the matter is that there simply is not a whole lot of research that verifies the existence of Silent Sabotage. The federal government does not monitor Silent Sabotage, nor does it investigate potential links between anemic values and their destructive influence on organizations. Likewise, there are no think tanks in Washington or New York that analyze the prob-

---

[4] Michael Crichton, *Jurassic Park*, Knopf, New York.

lem and propose solutions. The news media, outside of a few business publications, seems largely unaware of the situation. A great deal of anecdotal evidence exists about companies that are rebuilding their values (some of which you will read here). However, I can tell you from personal experience that re-evaluating and rebuilding values has been enormously helpful in providing me, my associates, and many of our clients with direction and a sense of purpose. At the same time, I'm seeing more and more evidence that the value of values is a concept that is starting to take hold all around us. Given time, I believe independent study and history will verify the benefits of sound applied values in the workplace.

It's also important that I state up front that *Silent Sabotage* is not a compendium about what's wrong with business, or society in general. Bookshelves are filled with too many chronicles of doom and gloom. I am not a card-carrying member of the doomsday crowd; I'm tired of negative media and depressed thinking. But I am for positive change. And, as you can tell from my picture on the jacket of this book, I'm anything but a leftover radical from the 1960s who longs to re-kindle a rebellion. I have spent more than thirty years working in business and advising people and institutions about what to do next and why. As a business executive, I'm also an optimist. You shouldn't be in business if you don't believe in the future. I believe that society has more opportunities going for it now than at any other time in human history. This book is about rebuilding and developing a clearer picture of our hopes, values, visions, and our principles, and restoring them to their rightful places in our lives. I am optimistic that we can once again become a nation of principles, and by extension, a world of principled people. It is my hope that our joy in accomplishment and public service will replace our passion for wealth. I also believe that it's time for all to reach deep down inside ourselves to bring about change—change that will stop the emotions that divide and separate us and that starts us on the road to realizing our greatest gift—human potential. Very idealistic, I know!

I do not bill my concepts or processes as instant panaceas. People will not make a conscious effort to do things differently unless they see value in change. But if we don't, I believe we will be swept up in a tidal wave of change that we have little influence or control over—much like the dinosaurs.

It is my hope that you will be able to use the thoughts and processes suggested here to improve your personal life, your corporations, institutions, and organizations. If you honestly feel that you don't have any major problems with values, then there's no need to continue reading. If, however, you believe that we are struggling to define our destiny, and that we are just coming out of an era when greed was our number one value, then you should read on. If you are really ready to challenge the "What's in it for me?" mentality that many of us currently live by, then I urge you to read further. And if you're willing to recognize that we are only as safe as our neighbors are safe; that we are only successful if other people have an opportunity to be successful, then you're on target.

At the very least, I encourage you to take a closer look at your own values and think about how they affect your life, your relationships with family members, business associates, and friends. Let's explore this challenge together.

1

America's Values Crisis

"It's no use saying 'we are doing our best.'
You have got to succeed in doing what is necessary."

WINSTON CHURCHILL

The best place to start considering values is with you. Let's begin with a couple of questions!

- Do you spend a great deal of your time alone thinking about what people are going to do to you or what you are going to do to them?
- Don't most of us spend a lot of time feeling either paranoid or egomaniacal?

If you answered yes, congratulations. You are a brave and honest soul. But take heart! You have plenty of company. Most people, when alone, worry a great deal about all the negative things that might happen to them or their loved ones. For example, if you spend a great deal of time worrying about how, or when, "someone is going to get me," or how bad everything is or is going to become, you've paranoid. Conversely, if you're constantly thinking about what you are going to do to others, such as, "I'll get them before they get me," or "I'll handle everything," you're an egomaniac. Answer these questions honestly:

- How much do you think about your career success and the negatives of your job?
- What about your boss? Does he or she appear to be on your side?
- How much time do you really spend thinking about the welfare of others?

Let's be honest. Even when we worry about our loved ones, do we think of their best interests, or are we really thinking of our own? Specifically, can you really think of other people without considering them in relationship to yourself? Will this relationship bring you more money? Will it make you look better? Will it enable you to get ahead? Or, "if I do this, will they love me more?"

Am I too tough on you? I'll confess that I too, came up with some of the sad, self-condemning answers about myself! Perhaps you are more charitable when it comes to thinking about others. I certainly hope so!

First, a few more questions relating to trust and to personal values:

- Do you believe that the government officials who represent you locally and in Washington tell you the truth?
- Do you believe that your politicians truly represent you and your best interests?
- What about your friends? Are they candid with you, and can they be trusted to be concerned about your best interests?
- Are you more positive about life and its fortunes for you and your loved ones than you were fifteen, ten, even five years ago?
- Are your values centered around your family, friends, faith, and fellowship?
- Do you think your employer will take care of you for life, or even be honest with you about your future?

If you find yourself answering no to all or most of these questions, you're not alone—some estimates say that seventy-five percent of today's employees don't trust management or even each other. In fact, our own *Drake Beam Morin* survey[1] of this issue in 1993 revealed some rather disturbing results:

- Approximately forty-five percent of the human resources executives that we interviewed believe that most employees distrust their own management.
- One in four employees believes that his or her current job could "end at any time." Not just change, but end.
- While sixty-seven percent of employees consider a "code of values" either "very" or "somewhat" prevalent among business, only seven percent think that most companies actually live by them.

Why the Fuss

Why such a fuss about all of these issues? Well, to change the direction of our lives, our nation, and the state that our institutions are in, we first have to change how we think about what is important to us. First, let's look at values.

Just what are "values?" Simply defined, the word *values* means "what is important to a person or to an institution." If you can't define what is important to you, it's pretty hard to give the emphasis to your life that's going to make it important to others, and of value to you.

Ask yourself, right now, what is important to you? Make a list of the five most important things in your life. Your list may include your children, your loved ones, their physical and mental health and overall well-being, and of course, your own well-being. Maybe you listed power or money—or even material things like a house or a car. Perhaps by digging

[1]"Values," Survey Drake Beam Morin, Inc., December 1993.

deeper, you tapped into feelings about your own achievements in terms of wealth and power and what you would define as personal success.

Let's think about it at an even higher level. How does striving for personal success and being involved with the needs of your own family relate to the needs of the larger "world family?" In other words, how do you balance your personal concerns about such issues as poverty, famine, and violent crime in the United States and throughout the world? What is your personal responsibility regarding the dictatorships, tyranny, and political oppression that exist around the world? Even in the United States, we may be victims of tyranny and oppression when local gangs rule the neighborhoods in small towns and big cities.

How do we resolve the problem of erosion of the rights guaranteed us in the Bill of Rights? How do we deal with difficult issues such as whether a minority has the same civil rights as the majority? And what about ethical issues involving the environment? Can we excuse companies, formerly thought responsible and reputable, that, we learn, knowingly dumped harmful chemicals into the environment? And what about companies in which responsible, educated managers actually knew that they were dumping chemicals that could kill.

The central problem, and the premise upon which I will build my case, is that for far too long our own personal values have been out of balance with the needs of society as a whole. And when that happens, the needs of the individual start to outweigh the needs of the many. When personal values become unhinged, it isn't long before society's value codes—the rules that govern behavior under a wide range of conditions—begin to crumble.

Pretty soon we find that the substance that once held us together becomes the material that pulls us apart. Eventually, we go from a world based on solid values to a world ruled by a *values crisis*.

What Is a Values Crisis?

A values crisis occurs when value perceptions become skewed; when we equate achievement only with making money; when our personal security is more important than those of everyone else; when we place a greater emphasis on making money than on serving customers. A values crisis occurs when we put "me" before "we." Many of us confuse a values crisis with economic or other crises. In the United States, for example, we've confused the values crisis with the health care crisis, the savings-and-loan crisis, the federal deficit crisis, or any of a dozen or so crises that compete for our attention every day.

At a presentation on the issues of trust and loyalty, I asked a business and academic audience whether our troubles today stem more from a values crisis or economics crisis. Many who heard me speak said that they felt that we have an economic crisis, which is causing us to question our values. (This tracks closely with a recent *Wall Street Journal*/NBC News poll that found that forty-four percent blamed our troubles on a decline in moral values, and forty-six percent blamed them on financial or economic pressures.[2] What do you think? Are economic challenges causing us to doubt our-

[2]NBC News/*Wall Street Journal* National Telephone Poll conducted June 10–14, 1994 among 1502 adults.

selves, *or* is the erosion of our values responsible for our economic downturn?

I believe that the prolonged worldwide economic downturn of the late 1980s and early 1990s was triggered by an erosion of values in the developed societies around the world. And to a large degree, this values crisis is responsible for all the other crises that afflict us these days—in business, education, real estate, and health care.

The Bottom Line: Values

How is this possible?

When you get right down to it, a crisis in values is really much bigger, and a great deal more serious, than any of those previously mentioned. Because if you peel away all the hyperbole surrounding each so-called crisis, you'll find the problem actually stems from an imbalance in our values. Did our education system simply fall apart, or did it simply fossilize because we failed to see the *value* of a strong education system? Over the last decade, did the real estate market bottom out simply because of the cyclical nature of the business or because we put too much false value into homes and properties? And did health care become a crisis because we cared so little about it for so long?

Some say that our values have been slipping away for many years now. The media may tell us that America "lost its innocence" after the horrors of World War II, the beginnings of the Cold War in the 1950s, the assassination of John F. Kennedy, the tumultuous 1960s, 1970s, and Watergate, and, finally, the rampant greed of the 1980s. No single event or happening or decade can be cited as the major factor. For example, the 1980s themselves did not cause values to decline. It was the cumulative effect of a long-term erosion that has come to a head today.

M. Scott Peck, in his recent book, *A World Waiting To Be Born: Civility Rediscovered,* calls our values crisis an "illness" that is spreading around the world; a basic lack of decency between people. He characterizes the disease in four lines from a Dun & Bradstreet ad that ran in *USA Today* a few years back. The ad featured a young executive on a business flight, and the copy reads:

> I'm thirty-thousand feet over Nebraska, and the guy sitting next to me sounds like a prospect.
> I figure I'll buy him a drink, but first I excuse myself and go for the phone.
> I call D&B for his company's credit rating. Three minutes later I'm back in my seat buying a beer for my best friend.[3]

These lines, as Peck so astutely notes, speak volumes about what we value and what we consider acceptable behavior these days. The old saying about art imitating life is certainly true here. The writers who created the ad and the agency that produced it certainly weren't born yesterday. They obviously felt that it was a realistic enough portrayal of an everyday business situation that readers would consider believable. There's not an ounce of compassion in the story, and yet this resourceful young executive is portrayed as someone to be admired and even emulated. And therein lies the problem: Is this the kind of behavior that *should* be put on a pedestal and emu-

[3]M. Scott Peck, Bantam, New York, 1993, p. 3.

lated? Should it be glorified in an ad? Or should it be held up as an example of unacceptable business behavior? And more to the point, is this really the kind of behavior we want to value and emulate ourselves?

These are questions I've spent a great deal of time wrestling with. The answers are not as obvious as you might think. When I first read the ad, I thought, "That's not the way to do business. And that's certainly not the way I want anyone who works at our company to operate either." But when I backed up a step and asked myself, "How should the people at my company conduct business?" and "What is it that we stand for?," I began to struggle for the right answers.

The more I thought about it, the more I started evaluating my own values. How could I possibly determine what my company stood for unless I could fully discern what I believed in? Suddenly I wanted to know exactly what was important to me and what motivated me to do better. So I went back to the very questions that I posed to you earlier in this chapter and I probed them even deeper. I forced myself to come up with clear responses to these questions:

	No	Yes
• Do I *really think* of others without first considering them in relationship to myself?	❏	❏
• Do I *value* honesty and sensitivity above personal gain?	❏	❏
• Do I *concentrate* on being the best person I can possibly be?	❏	❏
• Does my own personal success *come first* in my personal relationships?	❏	❏
• Is getting ahead *more important* to me than doing the right thing?	❏	❏

If you asked yourself these questions and answered "no" to a majority of them, as I did, then you already know my reaction and my dismay. (Obviously, "no" is the preferred answer for the last two questions.) My own responses shocked me. The plain truth of the matter was that I had lost sight of my own values. How could this be? I was raised on a foundation of family, faith, and fellowship. I was instilled with strong sense of right and wrong. Like many of us, I was raised by a code that said never to steal, lie, or cheat. It said honor your parents, and to do the "right" things.

I don't remember ever abandoning these values and beliefs. Yet years later, when I put them all down on paper, I had a hard time finding them at work in my day-to-day life. As it turned out, my values and actions were no better than those of that seemingly shallow guy in the Dun & Bradstreet ad. Unfortunately, I think my experience is fairly common. Most of us are basically good, honest people. We were raised on a clear code of ethics, and we were expected to live by these rules. When given a choice between doing right and wrong, the vast majority of us would always try to do the right thing.

However, we also live in an age unlike any other in history. It's fast-paced and stressful, and we're constantly bombarded with personal challenges. And stress doesn't always bring out the best in each of us. It's easy to be persuaded to do wrong, even when we've been taught otherwise. Consider Charles Van Doren, a main character in the quiz show scandals of the 1950s and the movie *Quiz Show*. He was a brilliant scholar and professor at Colombia University. Yet, when television producers told him that it was "okay" to cheat, because by doing so, he would be a model of higher education for children, he succumbed to the pressure. And Professor Van

Doren's case is mild compared to many of today's scandals; that in itself says a lot. We've been watching scandals parade by us for more than forty years. And in that time we've become more cynical, alienated, and insulated. Silent Sabotage has been gnawing on us ever since.

Whatever the cause of this values crisis in my case, it became painfully apparent that I had to do something to refocus and reprioritize the things that were most important to me. So I asked myself a simple question, "What is important and what do I really want out of life?" Coming up with the right answer was not nearly as simple.

I made a list and looked carefully at what I had written— I wanted health and happiness for my children and for my immediate family. It would be a great comfort to know that not only were my children physically and mentally healthy and financially secure, but were also capable of making a contribution to society. I also wanted my friends to be happy. As I was writing and then reading over my list, two things struck me. First, a lot of what I was writing had nothing to do with money. And second, I wasn't being honest with myself. Something was missing. I thought about it and went back to the list and wrote:

> I want success, and I want to make major contributions to others.

I sensed that I was getting closer to the truth. But I still had this nagging feeling that something was missing. So I pushed it even further. And as silly as it sounds, what I finally admitted to myself was that I wanted a sense of inner peace and contentment with what I was doing in life. But could I achieve this?

I knew that "winning" never equaled success. It wasn't enough. Also, success had to mean more than just financial success. I wanted something that was more complete, more substantial. If I could determine what it was that gave me a more complete feeling of success, I could then begin the process of piecing together my new code of values. Finally, after much soul searching, I determined that in building my new value code that I had to re-fashion my understanding of the meaning of success. I had to redefine success in terms of my relationship to my family, my ability to interact with others, my work and company, my friends, neighbors, my country, and the world. Simply put, I finally realized that if I could attain a sense of inner peace in most aspects of my life, then I would feel successful. This really isn't a new idea. Religious doctrines and philosophers have said much the same for centuries. But *how* do you do it? To quote Shakespeare, "Therein lies the rub."

A Personal Ethics Code

Out of this exercise, I developed a personal ethics code. The first step was to identify a code of ethics that I believed would give me the success which I now defined as inner peace:

1. To be honest, with sensitivity.
2. To think of the other person's motivation, needs, and desires first, before making judgments or even offering observations.

3. To concentrate on producing quality services or products with my work and leisure time rather than self-serving activities.
4. To take responsibility for all of my life's challenges rather than blaming anyone for them.
5. To persevere for the common good, no matter what the personal cost.

From here, I asked myself which value corresponds with each ethic. Here's what I came up with:

Values Code	Ethics Code
1. To be honest, with sensitivity	Respect
2. To consider the needs of others	Being selfless
3. To provide quality services and products	Contribute to society
4. To take responsibility for my challenges	Love of family and friends
5. To preserve the common good	My vision of what needs to be done.

Today, these five elements constitute my *personal code of ethics.* They hang on the wall in my office as a constant reminder of what I think is important, what I see as success, and what I must do to ensure my own sense of inner peace.

Some might think it funny that I'd go to such lengths, but I don't feel that way. No day goes by when I don't refer to the list. It's had that great an impact on my life.

At no time during this endeavor did I forget that a spiritual philosophy is also helpful in attaining a level of success. However, regardless of how spiritual you are, I believe a personal ethics code will help you in finding your own inner peace.

To be sure, I value the health and well-being of my children first. But in reality, I have very little control over that issue. I also want my company (and, of course, myself) to thrive financially, but this will only come about if I do the other things on my list. In essence, I have to place value on what I can mostly influence—me and my values. My friends and my children will have a better chance at happiness if I succeed in putting my own personal value code into action.

These goals serve as my guidelines for the future. I refer to them everyday. I've given copies to my family. I feel successful when I'm achieving the goals that these guidelines have set for me. Moreover, they are also helping me to achieve the balance that I need in my life and the assurance to know that in these times of doubt, I'm acting with the right intentions and striving for that difficult-to-attain "inner peace."

Now it's time for you to rediscover yourself. Let's apply the same exercise to you. Be very honest with yourself. First, list the most important values in your life. If it's power or money, list it. List the things that really make you feel successful, and rate how successful you are in attaining them on a daily basis. To do this, assign to each value one of the following ratings:

1. Successful
2. Partially successful
3. Unsuccessful

What we're trying to determine from this exercise are your true feelings about success. If you find that your list contains a lot of *1*s rejoice. You know what success means to you. But if you see more *2*s and *3*s, then you've got a problem. Most people fall into the latter categories because they really don't feel successful. They may equate personal success only with financial success. They look at their bank accounts, their cars, and other material possessions for proof of their own self-worth and achievements. But deep down, they're unhappy. Why? Because many people don't take account of the truly human values that contribute to an overall feeling of well-being and happiness. It's really a case of looking at the picture frame or the trappings of success without seeing the picture itself—what it is they value. More important, they're not seeing the details of the picture either. In other words, for most of us, the old W. C. Fields line still rings true today: "Money can't buy happiness, but it can make you comfortably miserable."

Look at the results of this exercise. They say something about what makes you happy. For most people, a sense of achievement or accomplishment is a primary component of their ethics codes. There's nothing wrong with that. It's when financial success *overshadows* other more meaningful measures of success—like the development of personal relationships or the satisfaction that comes with doing a job well—that our ethics codes become unhinged.

Deep down, I believe that each one of us have values that are just waiting either to be rediscovered or discovered for the first time. By pinpointing our personal success factors—attributes like health, mental well-being, and the success of our loved ones—we can begin to reprioritize our individual values and collectively get ourselves and others back on the right track. It's sure working for me!

And that's what the rest of this book is all about—identifying the causes and symptoms of weak values, identifying and prioritizing the factors that drive personal values, rebuilding shattered value systems, and setting up a process that helps restore balance to our lives, and, in turn, to our organizations. It's an important step for each of us and for our futures.

> A tip: Write down your definition of success and share it with your friends, family, and even with business associates. Get their feedback. Ask them to do the same exercise. It can be a great starting point for the values revolution that I believe is coming.

Once you have written out your values and definition of success, write down your code of ethics that support your attainment of your values. In other words, your code of ethics is your action plan that helps you maintain your values.

2

Why Value Values?

"Some values are like sugar on the doughnut, legitimate, desirable, but insufficient, apart from the doughnut itself. We need substance as well as frosting."

RALPH T. FLEWELLING, AUTHOR

The search for substance, spirituality and meaning in life is as old as civilization itself. The ancient Egyptians, whom we admire for their ingenuity, worshipped their religious figures above all else; philosophy was the glue that held the Greek empire together; the Roman empire was only as good as its government (in fact, Rome's fall was hastened when its republican government fell victim to corruption and anarchy); during the height of the British Empire, the British valued many things, but none so highly as adventure, exploration, and enterprise; and the Japanese, at the height of their expansionist period, lived by a code of self-discipline, sacrifice, and destiny that still drives them today.

Each of these cultures couldn't have been more different from each other in customs and laws. Yet, each was held together by a common thread—a value system that focused on what was important to their society. Within each culture today, people still live by a code of ethics—written and unwritten rules that govern personal conduct and serve as the basis for decision making. For example, we have the United States Constitution, which was intended by the founding fathers to be a statement of our national values—or truths. Some are as straight-forward as clarifying what behavior is right and wrong; some as inalienable as truth, justice, and the pursuit of happiness; and some as complex as equal rights for everyone.

Many of these values lie at the heart of our dilemmas today. We may question their relevance, but rarely do we take the time to understand where they come from, what they really mean, or try to put them into a context in which they can be used in our lives.

Our search for substance must begin with the past, with values that we have inherited from previous generations.

Values in the Past

Let's turn the clock back more than 100 years. The United States in the 1890s was an agrarian society. The nation's economy revolved around ranching or farming. People lived far apart from each other, separated by vast tracts of undeveloped land. Work days were long and hard. Communications could take days or weeks before it reached outside the big cities to the rural areas. Families needed everyone to help out, and neighbors needed each other to survive in tough times. Lending a hand to the neighbors was as much a part of life then as using a telephone is now. When someone hitched up the horses and rode into town, it was customary to invite the neighbors along so they could load up on supplies. When someone's barn needed building, everyone in the community joined in to raise it. Business transactions were struck by a simple handshake. And people were judged not by how well they played the game but by how well they kept their word.

At the time, this basic honor code was part of the fabric of our society. Comic books now refer to it as "the American way," but in reality it was a way of daily life. It meant that if you saw someone in trouble, you stopped to help. If others were less fortunate, or down on their luck, you helped them out. If you were driving along and saw someone pulled over to the side of the road with a flat tire, you stopped and lent a hand.

When I was growing up in the Midwest some forty years ago, you could still see some of that same code in practice. I remember my mother belonged to an organization called The Neighborly Club. It sounds kind of silly today, but the purpose of the organization was to promote friendship and community spirit among neighbors.

You don't see many Neighborly Clubs anymore. People aren't so eager to get involved in one another's lives and problems. The irony is that as we've become more urbanized and are living closer together, we've actually become *less* neighborly. And the lines between right and wrong aren't so clearcut either. What happened to our basic honor code?

Of course, there are those who will argue that our ethics code was really more Hollywood hype than reality. There is some truth to that. I don't think American values were ever quite as wholesome as they were portrayed in Frank Capra movies. The difference today, however, is that our approach to using values in our lives fundamentally changed compared to a century ago.

Most of us are not working on farms today. Many of us have pressure-packed, stressful jobs. We sit in traffic jams for hours. The wonders of technology bring the world into our homes but make us feel strangely out of touch with each other on a personal basis. We're stretched for time. We worry that we don't spend enough time with the kids.

History has tempered our attitudes towards values as well. In the last thirty years we had front row seats to three major political assassinations, we waged a war of questionable intentions in Vietnam, and we were torn by civil unrest and a breakdown of moral codes. A president resigned because he acted above the law. The birth control pill opened the door to greater sexual freedom. Elvis Presley and the Beatles reshaped cultural norms and helped define the sexual revolution through their music. We watched the Challenger space shuttle explode before our very eyes. The Clarence Thomas/Anita Hill hearings reduced our process of government to the level of a soap opera. The O. J. Simpson saga brought new meaning to the term "Greek tragedy." Every week it seems as if a new celebrity, government official, business leader, or sports star is accused of wrongdoing or scandal.

The list of celebrities who have died from drug abuse continues to grow. Drive-by shootings are so commonplace, that comedians make jokes about them. And our laws are viewed with distrust and disdain rather than respect. In fact, it's common today to see sports stars—the most visible of all role models, in trouble with the law and with drugs, and even fighting with fans, referees, and each other.

As of this writing, major league baseball has been without a commissioner for more than two years. Conventional wisdom has it that the last commissioner—Fay Vincent—was fired because the team owners were concerned that he was becoming too powerful, and they feared that some of his decisions would affect their bottom line. Actually, Mr. Vincent appeared to be trying to elevate the values and status of the spot. While league owners paid lip service to his goals, their actions indicated that their primary concerns were TV revenues, licensing, and ticket sales. Today, baseball, along with other major sports, has fallen victim to a "profit and power at any cost" mentality. There seem to be few values in today's sports world. Instead, we have sports celebrities who seem to exist for endorsements and personal pleasure rather than the joy of the game. Bo Jackson tells us to "just do it." A half-crazed football referee runs around the country in sneaker commercials worshipping high-paid football stars. Basketball stars like Charles Barkley pitch foreign cars and ask us, "you got a problem with that?"

The bottom line is that today's fast-paced lifestyles, coupled with the instantaneous transmission of communications, have transformed our society. They've brought the realities of a not-so-perfect world into our living rooms. And when that happened, life quickly switched from first gear into overdrive. We've seen more of divorce, crime, educational failures, and more corruption than at any other time in American history. We, in turn, reacted by becoming a more callous, disillusioned, and shock-proof people. The result: Our basic value system, which served for so long as our social "shock absorber," soon became a casualty of life in the fast lane.

Values Today

So where are we now? The dictionary describes a *value* as a standard, a principle, or a quality that is considered worthwhile or desirable. However, it does not define what those standards, principles, or qualities are. Maybe that's because we ourselves don't know for sure. But one thing is certain— there's nothing standard in our personal values anymore. Like a popular jeans commercial, current values seem to be "loose interpretations of the originals."

In this "anything goes" atmosphere, we find ourselves becoming skeptics who desperately want to believe in something, but can't. Let's look at a few examples.

Faith

Studies tell us that most people believe in God. But who really follows their own religion anymore? *Time* magazine, citing Wade Clark Roof, a sociologist at the University of California at Santa Barbara, reports: "Increasing numbers of baby boomers who left the fold years ago are turning religious again, but many are traveling from faith to faith, sampling creeds, shopping for a custom-made God . . . the returnees are still vastly outnumbered by the 42 percent of baby boomers who remain dropouts from formal religion."[1]

Faith, of course, is a deeply personal issue. I bring it up not to persuade you to become more devoted to your faith, but merely to point out that the decline of values and the upsurge in Silent Sabotage comes at a time when organized, traditional faiths are struggling. By the way, when was the last time you visited a church or synagogue?

Sexual Mores

The effect of the erosion of personal values is present throughout our society. Any discussion of personal values must start with sex. I'm not an expert on sexual issues, but I can comment on how sexual mores have changed in my lifetime and on some of the larger issues that are behind the decline in personal values. Consider sex education. In all our efforts to educate young people about sexual mores, very little is provided to students that actually relates sex to personal values. Perhaps in this politically correct era, we're just afraid to say it: Sex is better with someone you love. This notion seems old-fashioned, it's not

---

[1] *Time*, April 5, 1993, "The Generation that God Forgot."

cool, and it's certainly not in keeping with the scenes we've grown accustomed to seeing on TV and in movies.

Yet, for all the attention that has been lavished on sexual issues, there has been hardly a whisper about the fact that sexual relations are enhanced immensely if there are genuine feelings between people. Shouldn't we be teaching our children that the real values of sex is that it is the most intimate act between two caring human beings? Shouldn't we be talking about all the attributes that two people have in their relationship that would enhance the sexual act?

When values and sex are not linked, we wind up with what we have today—a society that tends to look at sexual activities not in the gestalt, but in the more basic scope of animal-like behavior. We have become a people who value immediate gratification over longer-term relationship building. This is true in our corporate lives, our personal lives, and even in our expectations that problems should be fixed immediately. How very naive we are! We have become a "sitcom" society—everything must get fixed in thirty minutes or at least no more than sixty minutes.

Education

Education is another classic demonstration of our misplaced values. Our current educational system is over 100 years old. It was designed for an agrarian society that required time off every summer so children could help tend the family crops. For example, tenure often protects the poor teacher rather than the controversial teacher for whom it was designed to protect. Today, few students—beyond those in the earliest elementary grades—view their schools as providing them with a true learning process. As we get older, we look at school as a ticket that needs to be punched in order to get a job. Teacher pay scales are so low and work environments often so bad that we can't attract qualified instructors into the profession. Our students don't even compare well with students from other countries. When they graduate into the real world—a competitive, no-holds barred high-tech environment—they're unprepared to contribute in a meaningful manner.

What do we do about our educational system? Very little. Sure we talk about returning to the basics—reading, writing, arithmetic, and old-fashioned discipline. We do make movies about school principals who walk around the halls carrying baseball bats and bullhorns, but we do little to alleviate the real problems. That says a lot about how little we value education.

What we really need to do is look at education in a completely different light. If we were truly serious about education, we'd stop trying to fix the old system and begin building a new one. We'd pay teachers what they were worth, on a scale that's commensurate with business salaries, and then evaluate them on the products that they turned out—qualified students. Finally, we'd fire teachers if students didn't do well, and pay them more if they did!

We'd ask teachers to come up with action plans—professional codes of conduct that would guide them in their dealings with students and colleagues. They'd be role models. We'd change our educational requirements so that students would be tested on how well they actually learned, and not on how well they memorized facts. And we'd start training students for the real world, by teaching them skills that they could use in the 21st century. We would learn to reward motivation and interest as well as rote memory.

After health, what's really more important than our children's education? Shouldn't educational excellence be one of our society's top values?

Business

What about the values crisis in the business arena? When values are not linked to outcomes, business suffers like any other area. The evidence has been with us for years—insider trading, payoffs, and bribes have become so routine that we hardly pay attention to the headlines anymore. The effects of Silent Sabotage—the slow but steady erosion of values within our society, organizations, and institutions—have been eating away at our corporate infrastructures for a long time. Yet it is only recently that colleges and universities have begun offering ethics courses as credit requirements in business programs. For the longest time, there was virtually nothing in the academic world to challenge young people to think about and develop their own codes of ethics.

On the brighter side, more and more companies are beginning to adopt value codes. But still, the vast majority of American firms today have no formal statement or code that defines what values are important to them and how they should act.

Summary

These are but a few of the most glaring examples of how our national priorities are out of balance. Unfortunately, we can't spend our way out of the problems caused by Silent Sabotage. We have to correct the cause. The bottom line is that our institutional problems won't change unless we as individuals change. And until we do, we can't begin to restore the equilibrium and the substance that's missing from our society today.

So now that we've looked at an overview of the problem of Silent Sabotage, the next logical questions are: "Why should we care?" and "Where do we go from here?"

Let's find out.

3

What Happens
When We
Don't Care?

"Top management is supposed to be a tree full of owls—hooting when management heads into the wrong part of the forest. I'm still unpersuaded they even know where the forest is."

ROBERT TOWNSEND, BUSINESS WRITER

When Clark Gable uttered, "Frankly, my dear, I don't give a damn," at the end of the 1939 movie *Gone With the Wind*, something snapped in our nation's collective consciousness. It may have marked the screen debut of Silent Sabotage. Back then, it was so shocking to hear a word like *damn* on the screen that most of us missed its meaning entirely. But over the years the term's meaning seems to describe all of us. Today, there's no escaping the "I don't give a damn" attitude common in our society. We see it practically everywhere—in line at the Motor Vehicles Department, at the checkout counter in the store, in the service department at the local car dealer, on the phone when we're trying to straighten out a bill, at home with the kids, and, of course, at work.

Our conventional wisdom says the boss doesn't give a damn about us; the boss is out to cover his/her own hide. So it only stands to reason that we shouldn't give a damn about the boss, about doing a good job, and we shouldn't give a damn about the corporation. It's a vicious cycle, and once it starts, it's very hard to contain.

They why should we care? Sounds like a pretty silly question, doesn't it? Nonetheless, it must be considered if we are to change. Why should we care about how we do our jobs, how we treat each other, about our individual and corporate value structures, or about issues like quality and customer service when it's much easier to simply rationalize them away? We may rationalize: "The business was screwed up before I got there, and in all likelihood, it will be screwed up regardless of what I do."

Let's flip that question over and see what kind of answers we get. "What happens when we don't care?" It's the question that cuts to the heart of Silent Sabotage.

At the outset, it may not appear as if much will happen if we don't care. But given enough time, an I-don't-give-a-damn attitude will work its way through the fabric of our corporate, governmental, and cultural institutions like a cancer.

Let's be clear: According to Labor Secretary Robert Reich, we built more prisons in America in 1993 than schools. The dropout rate in our public schools is about 25 percent nationwide and approaching 60 percent in our urban areas.[1] However, these are more than just numbers. They are warnings that Silent Sabotage is spreading.

What Happens When Businesses Don't Care?

What happens to a business when we don't care? Given enough time, a lack of caring will paralyze an organization's ability to do business. It will promote the stagnate environment of the status quo and depress risk-taking. Already, we can see what it's doing to the caliber and quality of our business executives. We find an abundance of *caretakers* in command—executives who seek nothing more than to maintain the status quo by protecting what others before them have built—rather than leaders who care about improving the fu-

---

[1] Robert Reich, Secretary of Labor, speech at a meeting of the National Urban League, Washington, D.C., August 2, 1993.

ture of the organization. Many become aloof and out of touch with their employees. They buy into the old military axiom that it's easier for the general to send troops into battle when he doesn't know them intimately; therefore, it's easier to fire people when they don't know their employees personally. The result is often less involvement and a highly detached and isolated workforce.

And while that philosophy may help boost profits in the short term, profitable success doesn't usually last. A 1994 study by Gordon Group Inc. for the California Public Employee's Retirement System concluded that companies that involve employees more often in decision making boast stronger market valuations than those that don't.[2]

We also see plenty of financiers who own businesses from a distance and have no real interest in them beyond profit potential. This new breed of "slash and burn" executives often come into organizations to sell off the most profitable pieces and prop up stock prices. We also see plenty of "short-term turnaround specialists" who practice "spike movement" techniques that prop up next-quarter results at the expense of long-term gains. Who pays for this shortsighted thinking? We all do.

Are You Part of the Problem?

Moving down the ladder, you'll find managers and employees alike who are more concerned about protecting their own turf than doing a good job. Are you part of the problem? Whether you are a business leader, a manager, a team leader, or one of the rank-and-file, ask yourself the following questions:

[2]*Business Week,* Aug. 1, 1994, page 47.

1. Do I have any *real* friends—people I totally trust?
2. How many people do I know by name in my organization, department, office, team, etc.? Do I even care?
3. Can the people in my organization really be trusted?
4. Would staff cuts shore up the organization's financial performance next quarter?
5. Does the staff tell me what I want to hear, or are they quick to bring problems to my attention?
6. Do I know the receptionist in the lobby by name?
7. How much time do I spend wandering the halls, the production lines, or the shop floor? Am I an engaged manager? Is it really profit before quality?
8. What's my long-term game plan? Where does the company want to be next year, two years from now, even five years down the road? Do I care?
9. Do I know our customers? Do I know them by name, do I know what they make, the problems they face, and the people who work for them?
10. Does my definition of success match up with the company's and/or with my business associates?

If you struggled with the answers, then the problem may rest at your doorstep. You may think you're a caring leader, but the actual evidence may point elsewhere. The truth is that when business leaders don't care about factors other than profits, we wind up with companies that are gutted for the sake of short-term profits. We wind up with companies without spark—lifeless organizations with no spirit or potential. If you're part of the rank-and-file, then you may be silently sabotaging you own job and career.

Sooner or later, the best and the brightest workers leave or turn off and tune out. Those who are left behind are shell-shocked and bewildered. We call them "the working wounded." Often, we are so concerned about the people who have lost their jobs that we fail to take into account the damage that is left behind. Those who remain behind are often troubled, abandoned people who are utterly demoralized.

We know of one company where many employees who left voluntarily returned to work on a contract basis, often earning four or five times as much money without the grief and aggravation that comes with working full-time. Financially, it's great for these freelance contractors, but guess how well it goes over with the remaining full-timers?

Morale sinks. Cynicism increases. Productivity goes right through the floor. Business performance plummets. And eventually, employees *just don't care*. Steven Covey, author of *The Seven Habits of Highly Effective People,* in a recent interview, talked about what has become of many managers.

> "Many supervisors and managers have what I call a scarcity mentality. Their sense of personal worth has always come from a contest with the rest of humanity. They're threatened by competence around them. So for them, to empower somebody means to take away from their own power. They talk the language of empowerment, but when push comes to shove, they really don't want other people to have that decision-making authority."[3]

What happens when employees don't care?

Attitudinal problems are the most likely result, and these, in turn, can become the *most* destructive forces within an organization. Violent strikes—like those that occurred in

[3]Steven Covey, *7 Habits Report,* Spring/Summer 1993, p. 7.

the auto and steel industries in the early years of the labor movement—are rare today. Rather, it's much more sophisticated and deceptive; hence, the name *Silent Sabotage*.

It's not as visible as a strike or formal work stoppage. But over time it can be just as hazardous to the financial health of a business. Silent Sabotage is encompassing—it includes work slowdowns, absenteeism, turf battles, cooking the books, ordering the wrong parts, installing faulty parts, and tampering with products. And that's just for starters. There's really no limit to the amount of damage this kind of activity can inflict. We've seen plenty of cases where disgruntled employees sabotaged entire business processes, only to find that at some point, the entire plant has to be shut down because of these problems. It all starts with the issue of whether or not anyone *cares*—cares about what is of value.

Bad management, poor morale—what else is new? The cynics argue that we've had both for as long as business has been around. That's true. But rarely, if ever, have we had a time when business leaders are so unwilling to lead, or when both management and labor have been so polarized and so unable to work together as a team. It's the I-don't-give-a-damn attitude at its worst. And the only way things will ever change is if management and labor step up to their common responsibility and start thinking about the consequences of what they must do to make it work.

Setting the Stage

Before an organization can be rebuilt, management has to set the stage. First, by identifying and believing in values and championing their cause throughout the organization. And then by creating an environment in which values will thrive; a work place where employees feel a sense of control over their destinies, where they are actually the experts on their particular phase of the work process. That takes guts, vision, and the ability to resist the temptation to micro-manage.

Who says so? Federal Express Chairman Fred Smith, for one. Smith is a big believer in employee empowerment, and he has the results to back it up:

> For us, responsibility and decision-making must be pushed to the person closest to the job. As demonstrated by courier Stephanie Flores, leadership can surface in any corner, even in the most unlikely places— like the middle of a flood in southern Louisiana. Having been informed that the Post Office would not deliver until the waters receded, a Federal Express customer awaiting a payroll shipment assumed we would be experiencing similar problems. Resigned to the fact that she would miss her payroll deadline, she was amazed to see Stephanie wading through water up to her knees toward the front door.[4]

It takes a different kind of business leader to energize people like this. But as the Federal Express example demonstrated, it also takes a special kind of team player to make a values program succeed. At Levi Strauss, a company that has been at the forefront of values building, (and is profiled in Chapter 8), Louis Kirtman is a good example of what I'm talking about. Kirtman had watched for years as he and other black execu-

[4]Fred Smith, speech, September 1990

tives were passed by for top jobs while publicly, the company talked a good game about diversity.

Today, he serves as president of Levi's Britannia Sportswear division. Things began to change for him in 1985 when the company really started backing up its words with action. Kirtman was tapped to help rescue the unit. He has responded in a way that helped turn the division around, and he is now the company's highest ranking black executive.

Carolyn Stradley's story takes a different twist. Carolyn was born into Appalachian Mountain poverty. Her mother died when she was eleven. She and her brother lived in a hut and ate wild berries and rabbits to stay alive. Carolyn was married at fifteen and became pregnant before she finished high school. She started work as a secretary and continued to attend school. Carolyn's husband died, but somehow she managed to persevere. She continued her studies in construction engineering and started an asphalt paving business. When she went to the banks for money, the bankers laughed at her. But she didn't give up.

After five years of running her own company and supporting a family, Carolyn landed the largest contract ever awarded by the U.S. Air Force to a female-owned business. Today, Carolyn's company bills its clients more than $2.5 million a year. And Carolyn is spending a great deal of time helping other struggling women entrepreneurs succeed. Now that's leadership—in someone who rose from the very bottom to the top.

We need more executives like Fred Smith—leaders who have a vision for their organization and a game plan for carrying it out; business people who are more than just expedient and proficient with a balance sheet. We need leaders who change human resources for long-term strategic reasons, not short-term quick fix ones. And we need motivators who can fire up an organization and boost morale.

Employee Leadership

A values-based environment also requires people on the other side of the fence—people who not only light sparks but can deliver them. Without employee leadership, values alone won't affect the organization. So we need more people Louis Kirtman and Carolyn Stradley, who have the courage to see beyond current circumstances and the motivational ability to carry out their vision.

This means businesses will have to move away from the old Peter Drucker definition of management, (getting the job done through people), to one where management's chief job is to create an environment where people can work to get the job done together.

In a process filled with intangibles, this particular aspect is as concrete as they come. Without managers who can truly lead, the process of rebuilding values in business is doomed. And before you shake your head in resignation, don't automatically assume that your organization is as stubborn as an old dog. I know what you're thinking, "What is new about all of this and what really can be done?" Hang on. I've seen some amazing organizational transformations.

It happened at Cin-Made, a Cincinnati-based paper packaging manufacturer. In 1984, the company was on the ropes. Workers and management were at each other's throats. Things got to the point where everybody eventually realized that there would no future unless the labor-management adversarial role changed.

Cin-Made's CEO Robert Frey, speaking in Washington, told *USA Today* that he, himself, "was a barrier to change."[5] The solution was pretty radical for the entire organization. In exchange for a twenty-five percent pay cut, workers were given nearly total control of the company. At first, employees were skeptical. But less than a decade later, the company has turned the corner and is prospering. The walls between management and labor have been torn down. The company has a working environment where people feel like they can contribute. Subsequent interviews with employees confirm that the feeling is valid. Ideas flow freely, and they often are incorporated into work processes or products.

At Merlin Metalworks, a small manufacturer of bicycles and wheelchairs, management looks at labor as an intellectual equal. All distinctions between workers and management have been eliminated. "At Merlin, there are not people who do the thinking and who do the work," said President Ashley Korenblat.

Employees also have a responsibility in setting the proper stage for a values shift. While management holds many of the cards, employees play a big part. For example, as an employee you must realize that the only way to secure your job in the future is to perform better. You must ask yourself how can you do your job better and more efficiently, rather than blaming every problem on everyone else or on the inefficiency of the organization. You must really see yourself as

[5]Mark Memmott, "Clinton Listens to Firms That Work." *USA Today,* July 27, 1993, Sec. B, p. 2.

a leader as well. In the future, employees will essentially become the experts in their jobs or solely responsible for some portion of the process of creating goods and services.

Some business leaders react negatively to the suggestion that employees will step up to the plate, even if they are given the right conditions and tools to do their jobs. These leaders are out of touch with the people who work for them. They see labor as a force with limited potential, rather than a source of untapped strength. As Jack Welch, CEO of General Electric, put it: "We need boundaryless thinkers."

We know what happens when nobody cares. What happens when we do care?

Good things start to happen. Product quality improves. Production schedules are met. Costs come down. Efficiency increases. Customers start to benefit. And, as is the case at Cin-Made, an atmosphere of non-dependent trust begins to build in the workplace. Companies that have crossed this bridge say that for the first time, an atmosphere of true trust has emerged. This is a new kind of trust—a trust that is based on skills, services, commitment, and products, rather than on the dependent "cradle to grave" trust that served as the foundation of so many organizational relationships in the past.

Look at what's happening in California where GM and Toyota are working together in a joint venture at an old GM plant. A recent article in *USA Today* described it like this:

> "I detested management" at GM's Fremont, California, plant 10 years ago, said electrician Martha Quesada. The poisoned atmosphere ended up helping to kill the plant—General Motors closed it in 1982.
>
> But after the plant reopened as New United Mo-

tor Manufacturing in the mid-1980s as a GM-Toyota joint venture, hourly workers won great authority. The auto plant now produces two of the highest quality, best-selling cars: Geo Prizm and Toyota Corolla.[6]

An amazing transformation? No. It didn't happen overnight. It takes time to change a working environment—up to several years, in fact—before tangible results start to occur and the effects of Silent Sabotage disappear. But without the right soil to nurture them, values-driven relationships will never grow.

And that's a pretty good reason why everyone should give a damn. What other choice do we have?

[6]Mark Memmott, "Clinton Listens to Firms That Work." *USA Today,* July 27, 1993, Sec. B, p. 2.

4

What Motivates Us and What Must Change?

"Don't be a fool and die for your country.
Let the other poor dumb bastard die for his country."
GEN. GEORGE S. PATTON

I wish I had a nickel for every time an executive compared business to war. How many times have you heard it in your own career—"We've got to execute the strategy!" Or, "if we all push the envelope—if we beat the enemy—victory will certainly be ours!" Sun Tzu's *Art of War,* which was must reading in the 1970s, succeeded only in reinforcing corporate battle cries with gems like, "If you know the enemy and know yourself, you need not fear the results of a hundred battles." Does this make any sense to you?

Let's get something straight from the start. Business—no matter how competitive in nature—rarely deals with life-and-death situations. Make or break, yes, but not life and death! Yet, ever since World Wars I & II, many American companies have gone about their business on a warlike footing. Think about that for a second. Many large companies are organized in a top-down fashion, with a formal chain-of-command that carries out instructions from the highest to the lowest level of the organization with no questions asked. These organizational structures are supposedly designed to do two things—beat the competition and preserve the organization at all costs. They are as rigid and formal as anything in a military textbook. And while military-style organizations may be great for winning wars, they're about as out of place in today's business arena as a horse drawn chariot.

Why? In war soldiers fight for territory, not for customers. However, in the business arena, customers can't be conquered. They live on and can continue to accept or reject you. When business operates in a warlike fashion, the people who really count—those who buy goods and services and those who depend on the organization and its employees—wind up as casualties.

If you have any doubts, just look at where the old command-and-control organizational structures have gotten us. Many industries—like consumer electronics and clothing manufacturing—have moved overseas. Other industries, like steel and high tech, are consistently on the ropes. In the last few years, the *Fortune 500,* the cream of American business, have laid off hundreds of thousands of employees. IBM, General Motors, and Sears—three blue-chip companies that once epitomized American industrial might and customer service—all grew so big, so focused on the chain-of-command, and so out of touch with reality, that they nearly put themselves out of business.

We all were surprised at how quickly these once great institutions became dinosaurs. In reality, there was nothing surprising or sudden about it at all. IBM, GM, and Sears each had dynamic, entrepreneurial beginnings. Each was once known for its great products and service. Each at some point adopted very formal, military-style organizational structures, and each lost an enormous portion of its business. Why? Because over the years these great companies (and others) lost sight of their most important constituents—their customers. How could this have happened? When you cut to the heart of the matter, I don't think these rigidly hierarchical structures ever worked well from the start.

What happened? To a large degree, we became victims of our own thinking. Companies held on to a paradigm that never changed with the times. Corporate America believed that bigger is better, faster is better, knowledge is to be kept, not shared, and money and position are all powerful. And everyone, from the highest ranking officers to the people in the mailroom, marched to the same drummer. We focused on financial results and not on quality and service. We concentrated on power. We lost sight of our real reason to exist. We valued winning over serving. We elevated companies and the titans who ran them to the point where they became almost God-like. Remember the famous scene in the movie *Network,* where the chairman of a broadcasting company, played by Ned Beatty, reads the riot act to the upstart anchorman, Howard Beale:

> You have meddled with the primal forces of nature, Mr. Beale. And I won't have it! . . . You are a grown man who thinks in terms of nations and peoples. There are no nations, there are no peoples, there are no Russians, there are no Arabs, there are no Third Worlds, there is no West . . . there is no America. There is no democracy. There is only IBM and ITT and AT&T, DuPont, Dow, Union Carbide, and Exxon. Those are the missions of today! The world is a college of corporations . . . the world is a business, Mr. Beale. It has been since man crawled out of the slime . . . and I have chosen you to preach this evangelism.

There's a lot of truth behind this satirical exchange. It wasn't all that long ago that industrialists actually envisioned an America where employees lived in houses that were owned and subsidized by their companies, and employees shopped in company-run stores. The General Foods headquarters in

White Plains, New York, is a good example of what might have been: This massive complex originally housed a barbershop, two restaurants, a small grocery store, and a shoeshine stand. Why even leave the building? Japanese companies like Toyota have taken this a step further—not only do Toyota's Japanese employees live in housing subsidized by their companies, but their children attend company-run schools, participate in company-sponsored sports, and the brightest of them are recruited at very tender ages as future employees.

This paternalistic strategy is designed to encourage blind faith and dependency among employees. It implies that you'd be taken care of with job security and a paycheck for life in exchange for your loyalty. And it worked—for a while. Many of us considered our military-style companies to be extensions of our families. But in retrospect, real paternalism was a promise that no corporation could keep. It succeeded only in stifling creativity among workers and producing myopic thinking in American and Japanese companies. It created a system in which bold thinking was reserved solely for the CEO or a few senior executives. It helped perpetuate rigid organizational structures. It rewarded caretakers, people who were dedicated only to preserving the organization, rather than moving it ahead. And it took the focus off customers and back onto the organization.

What did it do to us employees—the heart and soul of any organization? In a very real sense, we became docile slaves marching to the tune of a single drummer. We started telling our bosses what we thought they wanted to hear, not what was really important. In situations requiring moral judgments, we looked the other way. We followed all the rules, even those that made no sense, and very often helped perpetuate them. We didn't ask, we didn't challenge, and we didn't think about the consequences of what was going on around us. Thirty or forty years ago nobody would have believed that a chemical company would dump toxic chemicals into the Love Canal. And nobody even questioned the existence of the dump site. We wouldn't have believed that a car company would produce a vehicle that was unsafe to drive at *any* speed. And we wouldn't have questioned the nutritional benefits of an ingredient in a diet soda.

We know a lot more now and we operate in a completely different world. Fifty years of scandals, assassinations, layoffs, and a decay in values have led us to question everything from the ingredients listed on a box of cereal to the tax status of political candidates. Yet even in this age, many corporations are still operating with organizational structures, attitudes, and ethics codes that are as outmoded as Model Ts. And many of us have marched right along, playing the game.

Think about it in terms of your own experience:

- How much time do you spend thinking about what the boss or company wants to hear versus what's really best for the business?
- Does your organization really know its customers? How do you define your customers? Is your real customer someone you serve? Is it your boss? The shareholders? Or the people who pay for your products and services?
- Did the performance of your company last year justify the salary of your CEO and other top managers? Did it justify your own salary?

If your answers are typical of most American employees, you probably spend an inordinate amount of time worrying about what the boss wants to hear, not what he or she should be hearing. Your organization is so preoccupied with competing in the marketplace it doesn't have a clear picture of its customers; and if executive compensation was tied to performance, the CEO of your company might be standing in the unemployment line right now. More than anything, these answers illustrate that the old way of doing business is clearly not the right way to do business anymore. But with so much gone wrong, what can we do—both as corporations and individuals—to get back on the right track? Let's look at what motivates us!

The Road Back

There's no quick fix or cure-all to Silent Sabotage. But there are several things that we can do to get our organizations back on the right path.

At the organizational level, we must begin removing the hierarchical walls that we've built around us. We have to move away from close-ended organizations with independent departments that function in their own little cloistered worlds. We must move away from the concept that the boss is omnipotent and all powerful and move toward a more fluid organizational structure that favors a shared approach toward conducting business. Moreover, we have to abandon the belief that business is just a short-term proposition. It never was and never will be. Rather, we must fully embrace the notion that the only key to long-term success is true long-term customer satisfaction. Values and individualism must be prized, not hidden. In short, we have to expand our horizons and evolve from an internally focused view of business to an externally focused, customer oriented view. This means more than just reorganizing the business or reshuffling the players. It requires a whole new way of thinking about what we do and how we act.

So how do we get started?

Forget about the organization for a minute. We must begin by refocusing on the customer. Focusing on the customer is not a new idea, just one that everyone talks about but no one seems to understand.

A lot of managers suffer from "tunnel vision" when it comes to customers. They see them only as the people at the very end of the chain—the people who actually buy the product or service. Look more closely at the people who depend on what you provide. The reality is that there are many clients: Employees, trainees, suppliers, shareholders, surrounding communities, and finally society at large, that count on the products and services you deliver and on the taxes you and your organization pays. Each client forms your entire customer base. Each separate client has their own needs. Each is equally important to your business and livelihood. And you and your organization have an obligation to completely satisfy each and every client. Some of our consulting clients are absolutely astonished when they see how broad a customer base really is. But these constituents have always been there. The really amazing thing is that we've operated for so long without recognizing their existence, or the need to devote the proper resources to ensuring that their needs are met.

What's next? Once we can define and visualize our customers, we must look for ways to serve them better. What constitutes success as it relates to each customer base? Unlike the lumbering giants of today, organizations of the future must be flexible and easily mobile in the way they serve customers.

Successful organizations will be characterized by spirited teams of cross-functional employees who are empowered to reach out to customers with the specific purpose of understanding their needs, and providing specialized support and service. These employees are empowered to develop new products, manage whole businesses, improve systems and work processes, and plan their own work schedules. They will use "virtual" staffs that rely heavily on outside consultants, contractors, suppliers, and temporary employees.

How will all this work? Through a newfound trusting relationship. One that looks to balance meaningful relationships and service rather than telling the boss what he/she wants to hear.

What helps build this trust? At the customer level, the traditional sales call is a good vehicle. In the future, sales calls will take on a whole new meaning. Customers will be visited not only by the company's sales force, but by engineers, marketers, accountants, planners, human resources, and research employees. Company accountants will be meeting with customer accountants to ensure that the billing process is properly understood, that invoices are user-friendly and truly representative of the services rendered. Production engineers will visit customers to make sure equipment designs are on target. The product management team will call on the customer to see that the company's products are in tune with current needs. And a needs analysis team will also visit the customer to assess future needs and expectations. The customer will belong to everyone, not just to a sales account person.

But none of this can happen without a major shift in attitudes. Everyone has to re-examine his/her role in different terms and think about what he/she can do differently. Teamwork must be considered on a global—not a local scale. Teams have to be able to operate both vertically and horizontally. Reward systems have to be restructured to provide incentives and rewards to teams, as well as individuals who want to serve, not just to those who are politically savvy.

Meeting the needs of customers won't happen if management is barking out orders like generals or if the CEO is perceived as the sole decision-maker and chief slave driver. By the same token, customer satisfaction won't happen if employees are always looking for ways around management. To succeed, these kinds of organizational structures must be true partnerships.

If you are a manager, you must recognize that you are no longer all-powerful because of your position. Rather, you must realize that power will stem from your ability to effectively develop cooperating teams that impact favorably on the customer. Even your vocabulary has to change. Terms like, *my group, my decision, control,* and *dictate,* must be replaced by *our team, coordinate, lead, persuade,* and *counsel.* Other terms, like *execute, direct,* and *lean and mean* will be replaced by *accomplish, team, coach, partnership, empower,* and *enlighten.* (There are hundreds of books and seminars about team-building. Take advantage of them.)

By the way, managers don't realize it but their vocabularies are often downright demeaning to employees. For example, employees are *not* "expendable." If you as a manager want to regain the respect of workers, you must treat them as a resource—a truly valuable resource. Remember, no partnership will work if one side is operating on a higher ego level than the other.

Management must be seen as an integral part of the entire process of producing high quality goods and services. Think of what it would mean if management and labor really adhered to the concept of serving customers rather than ending up as adversaries. Think of the time, the energy, and the money that's expended on labor/management strife today and what we would save if we all worked together on the same team.

Management Initiative

Management must take the initiative by acting as an agent for changing attitudes. Management must first set the example for acceptable behavior, and then take it one step further: Management must take the risk and initiative by setting a *vision* for the company that gives people a sense of where the company is going and where it wants to be. Management should also find someone within the organization to help define what is acceptable and what isn't by establishing an ethics code—a real code that operates daily and doesn't just look good hanging on a wall. Establishing this values code should be a process that involves everyone in the company.

The values code doesn't have to be a book, just a clear and uncompromising statement of what the company believes in and what employees should strive for. Too many executives believe that ethics codes statements are little more than window dressing. Nothing could be further from the truth. Ethics codes are critical—they drive mission statements, strategic plans, and effective results-oriented behavior for the whole company. They can be as simple as "We value success, diversity, honesty, and ambition." But they must come from *within* the organization. They cannot be imposed. Here's the code that we've developed at DBM.

DBM Shared Ethics

We are committed to the following shared ethics as colleagues, striving constantly to translate these values into our work with our clients, colleagues and communities. Honesty and Integrity. We stand by our word, consistently and rigorously following through on all commitments.

- Respect for Others. We cherish diversity and respect each individual's need for a balanced life.
- Personal and Professional Excellence. We manage our individual careers and lives according to our highest personal and professional standards. We encourage challenge, risk-taking and life-long learning as vital to creativity and excellence in all we do.
- Open Communication. We speak our hearts and minds and share information on a timely basis to build trusting, productive relationships. We listen with sensitivity to others' viewpoints, making every effort to hear—rather than judge new ideas and approaches.
- Good Corporate Citizenship. We resolve to be good corporate citizens—making a positive difference in the communities we serve around the globe.

We'll look in more depth at how this code was adopted later on in this book. But for now, let me say that many of our client companies have adopted similar versions as part of their own organizations. Our code is not unique. The Ritz-Carlton Hotel chain, for example, has a credo printed out on small wallet-sized cards for employees. It states: "The Ritz-Carlton Hotel is a place where the genuine care and comfort of our guests is our highest mission." The credo spells out, in very detailed terms, the company's dedication to service and the steps it takes to ensure that its service is first rate. In addition, every department in every hotel writes its own statement. It states what is important—a true ethics code!

Some companies have fun in the process—Ben & Jerry's, the Vermont ice cream maker, has their values statement printed on a cube. PSE&G's electric business unit created a values-based shaving kit. Each kit contains a pen and a set of disposable razors. Each razor is emblazoned with one of six core values. The pen has a transparent window that showcases a new value whenever the pen's button is depressed.

More and more organizations are claiming that values have played critical roles in changing the attitude and character of their organizations. Hanna Anderson, a Portland, Oregon, company that sells children's clothes by mail, boosted sales and corporate loyalty by following through on its promise of social action. The company developed a program called "Hannadowns", which gives customers a twenty percent credit for mailing back clothes their children have outgrown. The clothes are cleaned and distributed to needy families or to women's shelters. The company has centered a television advertising campaign around the program. (We'll talk more in Chapters 5 and 6 about developing a code that's right for your company.)

Labor's Role

Hanna's program, like so many other successful plans, is not only driven by a strong commitment from management but by the enthusiasm and support of employees. For attitudes to truly change, labor must do its part too. Employees have to realize it is their absolute obligation to tell management what's wrong and what's right, rather than telling them what they want to hear. To be blunt, we can't afford to be ass-kissers anymore. This means thinking about problems in terms of solutions, not insurmountable obstacles. It means questioning orders, and when appropriate, suggesting better ways. It means taking responsibility for the pieces of the process that you control and doing everything you can to see that the job is done better, more efficiently, and to the highest possible quality standards. Finally, it means getting to know your customers. It doesn't do a company much good to define the customer if employees never meet the people who are on the receiving end of their products or services.

For some employees, the idea of getting out of the office and into the field will seem as foreign as a two-dollar bill. But without a willingness to experiment and try things differently, nothing will change. Employees take notice: You have to be open to new ideas and welcome opportunities to work with those outside your own traditional realm of contacts. On paper this looks easy. Who wouldn't welcome a more open, contributory environment? But when you're used to doing things one way for many years, there's bound to be some uncertainty.

Managers can help facilitate this transition by becoming better coaches and by encouraging their people to contribute in new ways; with ideas, suggestions, and support. Lee Iaccoca's old axiom—"Lead, follow, or get out of the way"—holds especially true for managers. In many companies today, managers are viewed as spineless jellyfish who are more concerned with playing politics and furthering their own careers than with supporting their own people. That's got to change. If you are a manager you have a unique role to play. Every good team has a good coach. They work hard to get the most out of their people. They facilitate. They encourage. They don't stand in the way. And they let their people fulfill their own potential.

Managers who become obstacles to progress will eventually find themselves removed from the process. If nothing else, American companies in the 1990s have learned to live without middle management. That should be incentive enough for any manager to think twice about what he or she is doing.

The New Team Management Approach

Believe it or not, there are plenty of companies today that are successfully operating on this new team management approach. We don't hear as much about them because they don't capture the lion's share of bad news. I'm speaking, of course, about companies like General Electric, which has completely transformed itself from a top-heavy conglomerate into a nimble, leading-edge competitor. At GE, Chairman Jack Welch tells people he's only as good as the receptionist who answers the phone and the hourly worker in the plants, and he means it. And I'm also talking about companies like Disney. Next time you're in a Disney theme park keep your eyes out for a building called Central Casting. It's not for actors, but for the employees who work in the park. They are considered cast members, not simply hired hands who run the rides and punch tickets. Each is well-coached on park operations and the Disney legacy. And each is committed to ensuring that customers have a great time when they visit the park. No detail is overlooked, from touching up street lights, to giving directions and handling medical emergencies. And the results speak for themselves. Disney's theme parks are unquestionably the finest in the world. And this spirit of customer satisfaction spills over into every other facet of the company's operations—movies, animated features, and retail stores.

Ford Motor Company used team-based development to redesign its 1994 Mustang, with impressive results. By relying on the contributions of employee teams, costs were cut by thirty percent over previous redesign methods. Ford calls its process "world class timing." It speeds decision-making and eliminates problems at an earlier, and less costly, stage.

Not every effort is automatically successful. The *New York Times* recently reported that companies like Bausch & Lomb and Dow Chemical have experienced transition pains in their efforts to move towards team management. Both companies had to grapple with turf rivalries between departments, they had to fight off traditional schools of thought, and deal with managers that balked at letting employees make decisions.

In these and other cases, the *Times* reported that problems often occurred when companies lumped diverse groups of people together and expected them to automatically develop the spirit and drive of a professional sports team.

It doesn't matter if it's football or manufacturing—diverse groups must first agree on a single goal before they can work together cohesively. Management must place a priority

on a team approach before they can expect to see positive results. Meanwhile, the transition to a team-based management
style can be more difficult than it appears. Not every company
can expect to become a Disney or GE overnight. But they can
be a lot different from the way they are today. Embracing a
team approach is a good beginning. Setting up an organization and methodology that encourages customer service and
high quality is the next step. Changing attitudes is arguably
the most difficult part of the process. But when we put these
steps all together—and begin thinking and acting differently—
then we are finally taking a big step in the right direction for
customers, employees, shareowners, and the future of our
businesses. Reengineering value systems will set the stage for
these changes to occur.

5

How to Rebuild Values in Your Organization

Step 1 in the Rebuilding Process

Up to this point we've focused on the dynamics that are driving today's values crisis and the underlying fundamentals that must change before we can address the rebuilding process. (If you're like most readers, you probably have a nagging suspicion that Silent Sabotage is no longer silent in your organization.) Now we move from the problem to the solution, as it relates to your specific organization.

The first order of business is to determine beyond a reasonable doubt if, in fact, your company is suffering from Silent Sabotage and what should be done about it. We begin by closely examining and analyzing your situation and taking stock. I should note here that Chapters 6 and 7 include several surveys, exercises, and questionnaires that are designed to help reengineer values. This chapter contains two surveys, and I recommend that you take time out to complete them and then carefully consider the results. When you finish this chapter, you should have a more complete picture of how both you and your organization perceive success and where your own priorities lie. When you are finished with the entire discovery process, you will have a better sense of where your organization's values are and what must be done to rebuild them. Specifically, you should know:

- Whether or not your company's values are balanced.
- If your company's values are out of alignment, you should be able to gauge how bad the problem is.

- Whether or not Silent Sabotage is taking place.
- And finally, how well balanced your own personal values are.

Let's start by asking ourselves the obvious: "Should we rebuild or revisit our value code?" It's still early in the discovery phase of the process, so few could answer with an unqualified "yes." (However, if you can, go to the next chapter.) The reason: Most organizations need more solid evidence before proceeding. That's only natural. It's also natural to encounter a large dose of skepticism, particularly in larger, poor-performing, bureaucratic organizations to this entire process. Put another way: Be prepared for those who seek to preserve the status quo.

Leaving Well Enough Alone

Let's consider one such scenario. Suppose things are sailing along in your organization. Profits are fine and sales are up. Why not just leave things the way they are and let events fall where they may? If we were all living in a vacuum, this might be a course worth considering. But as much as we'd all like to live in an environment that's completely tranquil and painless, the truth is that we will never survive in a world that resists change. Change will occur anyway and manage us if we don't have some say in the way the future unfolds. History is filled with tragic examples of what happens when organizations stand by while change takes place around them. Bell & Howell is one such case. In the late 1970s and early 1980s, the company sat idly by as video recorders made the home movie market obsolete. Xerox is another classic case in an organization that sat on its thumbs while the Japanese grabbed the lion's share of the copier market. The company nearly went out of business. Then there's IBM. Who could have imagined a company like IBM giving away the software business to upstart companies like Intel and Microsoft? Likewise, who would have believed that CBS—once hailed as the "Tiffany Network"—would someday lose the rights to broadcast National Football League games, along with several important affiliate stations around the country, to an upstart network like Fox?

On a larger and more important scale, consider what happened half a century ago when Hitler's promises of non-aggression lulled the European continent into a stupor: A false sense of security set in, and it eventually led to World War II. But look at how different the outcome was just a few years ago when the nations of the free world drew a line in the sand in Kuwait and stood up to a ruthless dictator before he could shape world history.

Once again, we're not applying military techniques to business problems. The main point is that events *shape us,* unless we *shape them ourselves.*

In business, *complacency* is an early warning signal of Silent Sabotage. How do you know if you are at this point? How do you know if your organization is sleepwalking into disaster? Or maybe already knee-deep in trouble? It's time to take stock. First, answer the following questions about yourself and your situation:

1. Yes___ No___ Do you think the growth of your firm is broad based, or does it have all its eggs in one basket?

2. Yes___ No___ Do you feel there is enough balance in your life between personal and career growth?

3. Yes___ No___ Do you honestly think you have solid communications with loved ones and friends?

4. Yes___ No___ Do you think that your peers and those who report to you at work would say that you pay a great deal of attention to their ideas and suggestions?

5. Yes___ No___ Do you feel you have a reasonable picture of what you'll be doing five years from now?

6. Yes___ No___ Do you spend up to twenty-five percent of your time helping people progress in their lives—people other than your own children or loved ones?

7. Yes___ No___ Is your company really more involved today than it was five years ago in trying to improve conditions in society?

8. Yes___ No___ Do you feel comfortable that you know enough about the personal value of colleagues—the special qualities that they bring to the picture?

9. Yes___ No___ Do you feel you are more skilled at your job or are you more politically astute?

If you answered "no" to six or more questions, then something's out of whack. It's hard to say precisely what's wrong with just one exercise. However, it appears as if priorities—either in your situation or in your company—are out of balance. Is this enough to justify redefining values for your organization? No. It's a good start, but we need more evidence.

As individuals, developing new values (or redefining old ones) is really a matter of personal choice. But for business, developing new values isn't so clear-cut. If management in your organization hasn't focused on values in a long time, chances are nobody knows for sure what is important to the organization and what isn't.

Remember the old "Honeymooners" episode where Ralph Kramden decided to become a "new man?" He lists all the characteristics that he'd like to emulate and puts a check mark next to each one as he achieves it. To avoid losing his temper—one of Ralph's biggest faults—he recites a little rhyme—"Pins and needles, needles and pins, it's a happy man that grins."

Ralph's exercise didn't succeed, because in the process of trying to recreate himself, he suppressed all of his best characteristics—the qualities and values that people admired most about him. By the same token, businesses can't throw the baby out with the bathwater either because it may discard some of the values that are critical to its success. It's a frustrating situation. How do you determine if values must be rebuilt if there are no guidelines on pinpointing whether or not current organizational values are on target?

Early Warning Signs of Silent Sabotage

Organizations suffering from inadequate value systems often send out their own early warning signals. We've already discussed complacency as a sign of misaligned value systems. But that's really just one piece of the overall picture. Warning signals come in a broad range of guises—from performance to communications. Few, however, see these signals as part of a larger pattern or problem. For example, if sales are slipping, we're not pushing the sales force hard enough. If inventory is backed up, the financial planners are doing a poor job. If the annual employee survey shows management up and down the line is inadequate, then either management isn't communicating or the workforce isn't listening.

Consider the following questions and apply them to your own organization:

- Are sales slipping?
- Are profits eroding?
- Has the stream of new products slowed to a trickle?
- Do labor costs represent an inordinately high percentage of operating costs—higher than your competitors—even though your company has made a concerted effort to reduce payroll levels and improve productivity?
- Is the company's vision clear?
- Is the direction of the organization confusing?
- Is the grapevine the most influential source of communication within the organization?
- Do new ideas flow easily from the staff?

If many or all of these questions are difficult for you to answer, it's likely that company values are weak or even non-existent. It's also a good bet that Silent Sabotage is slowly draining the life out of your company.

Next, look inward—at the people around you. If your organization's performance isn't what it should be, chances are your people know it and they're acting the part. People are behaving differently, and the signals, while often subtle, can be identified with little trouble. We call these the "Eight Signs of Silent Sabotage":

1. *Employee theft on the rise.* People who'd ordinarily never take a pencil are helping themselves to supplies because they feel they've been abandoned by the organization.

2. *Stay-and-quit syndrome.* This occurs when employees leave their spirit, enthusiasm, and desire to get things done at the front door. Often it comes down to the point where nobody will go the extra mile or even an extra step.

3. *They're out.* Some employees, particularly the high performers, will decide that the floorboards are too shaky and will use much of their time thinking about and actually looking for their next job. When this happens, they're often as good as gone.

4. *The water cooler gang.* An extra coffee break to seek and share more company gossip can be deadly to all concerned. This often results in lost hours for not just one, but several employees, since this activity is rarely done alone.

5. *Huddle and chatter.* In times of heavy company stress, you'll notice people gathering and chatting very quietly and privately about what has happened and what might happen. It's less public than the Water Cooler Gang, but almost as obvious. The results are similar—untold hours of lost time per week.

6. *The diverters.* These formerly faithful employees will actually divert business away from your company by not responding to, not acting on, or by entirely avoiding business opportunities.

7. *The spendthrift.* The staffer who once watched the com-

pany budget as if it was his kid's college fund now spends without restraint.

8. *The clam.* This bright, productive person suddenly stops saying or doing anything creative for fear of being wrong, judged harshly, or even passed over for promotion.

These are all indicators of serious values erosion. Think of them as values barometers. Individually, they characterize the behavior of employees. Taken collectively, they say a great deal about the state of values in your organization. The more signs you discover, the deeper the problem.

Every organization is different—you may see more of some signs than others. We do know, from past experience, that these characteristics are typically found in companies that are restructuring, downsizing, and struggling.

However, this doesn't mean that successful companies are immune to values erosion. One very successful consumer products company—which was profiled recently in a best-selling book—also comes to mind. According to the book, the company did plenty to destroy employee values on its own. How? By firing employees for leaving company phone books on their desks, and by placing company security guards on planes to ensure that their own advertising executives didn't talk shop while flying to New York or Chicago.

It's hard to believe that in today's high cost business environment that any company would have the money to spy on its own people. But I've seen plenty of other examples of corporate self-destruction. One Fortune 500 company, for example, made it a practice to place phony blind want ads in major metropolitan newspapers to see how many of its own employees responded. This practice continued for years. At no time did it dawn on senior management that their own employees might eventually discover the ruse (they did). And no one would have thought that the money could be better spent building an environment that would be more conducive to success.

The lesson here is that values erosion can be triggered by economic conditions, management attitudes, the organizational structure, employees, or a combination of any of these elements. The fallout is almost always the same, regardless of the circumstances—values erode, performance declines, and eventually, the organization starts to unravel from within.

DBM has developed the following guide to detect these early warning signs and provide a clearer picture of the state of values in your organization. Consider the following about your organization:

- *Perceptions.* Do employees have a sense that something isn't right about the organization or its business?
- *Language.* Do people in your company really state it as it is?
- *Rewards.* Does your company reward constructive dissension, different points of view, and diversity?
- *Responsibilities.* Does your company make it an obligation for employees to tell management what's wrong?
- *Actions.* Does your company talk about how its value code has made it a more successful business, or does it just talk about values?
- *Management Style.* Does your company's management "walk the talk?" Does management deal constructively with managers who don't walk the talk?
- *Character.* Does your company have a reputation for being lean PLUS mean? Is your company considered hard-

nosed, insensitive, *and* uncaring? Is mean more often in the way of being effective and lean?

- *Communication.* Is your management closed-mouthed? Are senior executives aloof and distant? Does the chairman or president still believe in keeping a distance from the troops?
- *Organization structure.* Is your organization still based on a military, hierarchical concept? Remember, the new concept is that the structure should be so flat that it will slide under the door.

If more than half of these characteristics describe the atmosphere in your organization, chances are your company is experiencing a values drought and Silent Sabotage is sneaking up on you. The potential for disaster is great. And now, you should have an answer to the question that we asked at the top of this chapter: "Should your company rebuild values?" Let's take the next step and *do something* about it.

6

Seeing Success for What it Really Is

Step 2 in the Rebuilding Process

The most difficult step in determining values, as I've mentioned previously, is defining success on both an individual and organizational basis. I include both together, because many mistakenly assume that individual perceptions of success don't count and jump right to the organizational challenge. However, the relationship between individual and organizational perceptions is almost symbiotic—you can't have one without the other. In this chapter, we'll focus on how to define success both on an individual and organizational level. As in the previous chapter, we've provided a number of short exercises that are designed to help uncover attitudes about success. These exercises are part of a larger written package that we use at DBM when clients ask us to build values profiles for. When you are done, you will have a better sense of:

- The activities that make you feel successful.
- The achievements that you are most proud of.
- How you define success.
- How to use individual perceptions of success to determine whether your organization and its people are thinking along the same lines when it comes to success.

Again, I urge you to take time out to answer these queries and consider the results.

How an organization defines success hinges largely on

how the individuals in that organization perceive it. For example, let's assume that you have everything you want in life—plenty of money, automobiles, closets full of clothes, fame, and power—everything you've ever imagined. You're the president of a big company, the king of a country, a head of state, or maybe the president of the United States, and your supply of wealth and influence is endless. Is this success?

By our current Western standards, we'd have to answer "yes." This is what we work for, and what we spend most of our lives attempting to gain. But ask the person who's actually got all this power—particularly the head of a company—if he or she is happy and the odds are high that the answer will be "sometimes," or a resounding "no." Most say "something is missing." They say they feel unfulfilled or dissatisfied. Sometimes they crave more of what they've got. Very often, they don't know what's wrong.

Then there's the other end of the spectrum. When I was a kid, my parents led a very simple life. Success to them was wrapped around getting a paycheck on Friday afternoon. Their whole lives seemed to be focused on living for payday. I can tell you from personal experience that the two or three days following payday were always the most gratifying around my household. But as time wore on my parents grew more and more anxious waiting for the next pay period to arrive.

Many of us are trapped in this same type of hand-to-mouth existence. It may seem strange, but perhaps it's an easier existence than having all the things you want in life and thinking you've attained success. It seems that many people who are wealthy and powerful are no happier or pleased with their lives than those who live from paycheck to paycheck. Both groups appear unhappy.

Likewise, corporations have an even tougher time coming to grips with what constitutes success. When things are going well for an organization—sales are up, company stock is performing, and shareholders are pleased—yet, the people inside the organization are often unhappy. Complacency sets in. People get bored. Turf battles set in. Politics becomes the primary occupation for many. Others grow fearful of change. They see success as something that must be sheltered. So rather than taking chances, people pull back and protect their turf and their paychecks.

Isn't it strange that even when things are tranquil, boredom somehow creeps back into our lives? The same happens to organizations. Many companies get locked into routines and employees begin to be dulled by the sense of security that large corporations provided for so long for so many. For decades, companies like IBM and General Motors had achieved such a steady rate of growth and prosperity that it became routine and predictable for employees. As a result, they avoided risk. Quality and customer service suffered, and internal politics prospered. Protecting the status quo became more valued than charting new ground. Punching the clock became more important than serving the customer.

This is an important point because the ability to embrace change and see it as necessary and stimulating, rather than something to be feared, lies at the heart of developing a positive values system. When individuals perceive change with trepidation, eventually so do the organizations for which they work.

Defining success, therefore, should begin at a very personal and individual level. This requires a great deal of self-reflection and readjusting. Complete the following questions on success:

1. How does society define success?

2. How do you/will you know when you are successful?

3. List the actions/activities that make you feel contented:

4. List the achievements you are most proud of:

5. Now, write your personal definition of success and share it with at least five people. As you are writing, take into account the following factors:
   - Money/financial stability
   - Material possessions

- Health
- Family
- Career
- Contributions to society
- What is most valuable to you

If you're like most people who take this exercise, you'll be surprised to see how frequently terms like "contributing to society" and the notion of service to others keep surfacing, over material gains. When it's the other way around—when more people in an organization consistently cite material wealth over service, it's an immediate giveaway that something's not right in the values department.

Seeing the Big Picture

Let's put this exercise aside momentarily and consider the larger picture of success. We have to ignore what's been ingrained in us for so long—that life is a finite journey and we have to beat the clock in everything we do regardless of what it costs us while we're here. However, to truly achieve success, we have to realize that life is a continuum that exists after we're gone. While we're here, we have to serve that continuum, contribute to it, and improve on it for others who follow in our path.

If you apply this concept to a corporation, to its philosophies and mission, you'll also find that the purpose of the organization should be to serve and contribute on a continuing basis. Or put another way: A company should strive for the best performance possible on a continuing basis rather than to achieve short-term results. Deep down everyone knows this, but why don't we do it?

All too often in American corporate life, the top officers have gained wealth even when the corporation itself has lost status, wealth, position, and its ability to serve. Therefore, some individuals are served on a short-term basis, while the corporation suffers long-term losses because of individual greed and attention to power-building and brokering. What is the shared value here? Short-term greed is all I can think of. What about you?

The point of all this is that it's becoming increasingly evident that the objective for all of us is to serve—our customers, families, and our friends—and to focus on improving our ability to serve. That a fulfilling definition of success. I know it's not a new concept. For years we've talked about a "service economy" or a "service mentality." If we had done more than just talk, we'd actually be maintaining customer relations at all costs. In the process, we would be aiding our organization, and of course, we would be serving ourselves as well. Ultimately, we would gain a true sense of inner peace because we would be contributing to society.

I'm not talking about a religious experience. But history provides us with a great mirror—civilizations that have been based on taking, power-brokering, and pyramiding by individuals of income, wealth, and position—have left little to succeeding generations.

Let's continue with our exercise. The following are designed to pinpoint the factors that you consider important for establishing balance in your life. Answer the following to the best of your ability. When you're done, show them to a few colleagues and ask them to complete the exercise as well.

1. If your life were in perfect balance, how would you describe it? Identify the key areas (family, career, community, recreation, etc.) and note the "weights" devoted to each for maintaining perfect balance.

2. Comparing your life currently with your description of a perfectly balanced life, are there areas that are currently out of balance? If so, list them and explain why, if you can.

3. What action steps could you take *now* to achieve better alignment between your current life and your perfectly balanced one?

Study the results from this sampling. Look for an imbalance between the factors that comprise individual perceptions of success and values, and those of your organization. Often, it comes down to a *collision* between individual and organizational values. On the one hand, you may find an employee (in fact, many) who says her life would be perfectly balanced if she could leave the office everyday at 5 p.m., knowing her work was done and that her contributions were appreciated, without feeling guilty. But if your organization values employees who burn the midnight oil, then you know there's a problem. If someone says his personal mission is to create products that contribute to the well-being of the environment while fulfilling a need in the marketplace, and the organization is dedicated to producing products that fill a need at *any* cost, then the individual and the organization are not in balance with each other.

So the central question that each of us must ponder in coming to terms with success is: "Is it to serve, or to gain?"

At this stage, you should have a better sense of how you and your organization define success. So, we can make a few assumptions:

- If you have come to the conclusion that you and/or your organization value gain above all else, then you and/or your company have a distorted sense of success. This, by the way, is what our friend in the Dun & Bradstreet ad was driven by—gains, profit, and glory.

- If you have concluded that you and/or your organization value service above all else, then we can safely assume that there is a good sense of balance here.

Organizations that prize service before profit, often see it as a self-fulfilling prophecy. Commitment to service often leads to greater gains. Lexus is a great example. Every year it's atop the J. D. Power and Associates survey of customer satisfaction. It's not surprising then why Lexus is consistently among the top selling luxury imports in the United States.

This might surprise you, but I believe it's possible to have the best of both worlds. But not without a commitment to serve first. Let's begin rebuilding.

7

Making It Work in Your Life and Your Company

Step 3: The Rebuilding Process

"The value decade is on us. If you can't sell a top-quality product at the world's lowest price you're going to be out of the game."

JACK WELCH, CHMN.,
GENERAL ELECTRIC

Let's assume that after answering all the questions in chapters 5 and 6 we've come to the inescapable conclusion that our organization's values are in a state of crisis. Our definition of success is stilted. We value gain over service. We have a complacent workforce that mistrusts management. Few in the organization know what the company is all about, what it is trying to do, and what it stands for. Rebuilding is the only option. Part of you can't believe it, but part of you suspected that there was a problem all along. You're not alone. You're not crazy. And here's why. The case for rebuilding shared values has never been stronger. Consider what's going on at the national level:

- According to the American Management Association, every year since 1988, one third to one half of all large and mid-size American companies downsized their workforces.
- Of those companies, 80 percent reported that morale collapsed.
- Two-thirds of those companies showed no increase in productivity.
- Less than half saw any improvements in profits.
- Thirty percent found overtime costs increased.
- Twenty-two percent discovered they had eliminated the wrong people.
- Negative employee attitudes almost always affect customer attitudes.

- Our own DBM studies of the situation reveal a high level of distrust for management among workers across the nation. In fact, 70 percent of those polled in our examination say they can't trust management.

What does all this mean?

The results clearly indicate that Silent Sabotage is alive and well. At the same time, I think such evidence is the strongest argument yet that our corporate medicine of choice—downsizing—is not working. Trimming the workforce only succeeds in exacerbating the problem. From my experience, the second most popular option, "doing nothing," isn't helping either. The only logical alternative for companies that are interested in staying in business is to restore trust between employees and management.

Rebuilding employee/management trust based on a clear value code is a big undertaking—one that affects virtually every facet of the organization. It involves an intensive self-examination process, above and beyond what we've already done so far; an organization-wide effort to define what it really means to be successful, where the company wants to be someday, where it is now and how it goes about its business, and finally; a new values code and an action plan for successfully implementing it.

To succeed, the revitalization process needs leadership from the top, support from the bottom, and the consensus of everyone in between. To get there, we must strive to align both personal and corporate values. Here's what the process looks like in model form:

Draw a line that represents alignment. If you are in complete alignment then the line will be straight between your personal definition of success, and the company's definition. If not, then the line will be off; how much is up to you.

Personal	Success	Corporate
Define success	A	Define success
Values	L	Values
Balance	I	Balance
Vision	G	Vision
Mission	N	Mission
Directions	M	Directions
	E	
	N	
	T	

To measure this process in any other way would be like assembling a car in reverse order. It won't come out right. And it won't move forward. Each category must be balanced.

Rebuilding values should not be attempted alone. I say this not because my company helps clients develop shared values programs, but because I know from our own experience at DBM—see the case study section at the end of this chapter—that this undertaking requires expertise in organizational behavior and transition. Attempting this without that special insight will not only prolong the effort, but it will likely hinder it. I think it is also important to point out at this juncture that reengineering values isn't as systematic or as structured as filling out an order form or processing a payroll deduction. Values development is still in its infancy and is filled with intangibles. What works for one organization may not be right for another. So while we are presenting this as a step-by-step process, I must point out that development does not always follow a straight line.

Before anyone commits to this kind of effort, you've got to be sure of your facts. You've got to verify your own conclusions by going straight to the people in your organization. This means determining how deep the problem is; where the people in your organization stand; and then, if justified; begin the consensus-building process that will lead to change and further development of a values code. What follows are the steps in the rebuilding process.

Step One: Analyze the Situation

The process of building a shared values system is much like that of a scientific experiment. One avenue of investigation often leads to another and experimentation verifies theories and hypothesis. This applies to the analysis phase of the values rebuilding process. You've already gone through it in your mind. But just because you've come to the conclusion that values are out of whack doesn't necessarily mean that they are, nor does it tell you the depth of the problem if there is one. To paraphrase Yogi Berra, "It's amazing how much you can hear just by listening."

The first order of business is to find out as much as you can about the people in your organization—what motivates them, what they hold dear, and how they're reacting to your organization's direction.

Take the following steps:

A. Determine current values, expectations, and interests. Develop a communication form (it can be a simple questionnaire) or conduct question-and-answer sessions in small group meetings. Ask everybody in the organization to do the following:

1. List, in priority order, the values that are important to you in your pursuit of success. (Examples: honesty, fulfilling family relationships, religion, contributing to society.)

2. Develop your own personal code; guidelines that represent your values. Use Jack Welch's guidelines[1] as an example:

   - *Face reality as it is, not as it was or as you wish it were.*
   - *Be candid with everyone.*
   - *Don't manage, lead.*
   - *Change before you have to.*
   - *If you don't have a competitive advantage, don't compete.*
   - *Control your own destiny or someone else will.*

3. If your life were in perfect balance, how would you describe it? Identify the key areas (family, career, community, recreation, etc.) and note how important each one is to maintaining perfect balance.

4. Are there areas in your life now that you consider out of balance? If so, list them and explain why.

5. What action steps would you take now to achieve better alignment between your current life and a perfectly balanced life?

6. In those areas of your life where you identified an imbalance, are there some that could be changed by

[1]Noel M. Tichy and Stratford Sherman, *Control Your Destiny or Someone Else Will*, Doubleday, New York.

looking outward to serve rather than looking inward to take? If so, note each area and describe how you could change it to a more service-oriented focus.
7. What do you think your company's values are?
8. What do you expect from the company?
9. What does the company expect from you?
10. How would you define success for the organization?
11. How do you define success?

The last question is important. Have everyone in the organization—including top management—write out what how they would define success. As we discussed earlier in the book, personal perceptions of success are critical in determining values. In organizations where values have gone astray, the heart of the matter often boils down to confusion and inner conflict over the definition of success. Analyze the results and look for areas of polarization, and by the same token, areas of commonalty. You may find a great deal of non-alignment.

B. Find out what employees think about trust in the office, department, or organization. Trust cuts to the core of shared values; it is the cornerstone for building a shared values system. The following exercise was developed for middle managers looking at top management. It represents a first step in exploring the level of trust in your organization. A more complete discussion and evaluative exercises relating to this issue can be found in the *Appendix*. Ask managers to complete the following survey of descriptive statements about top management. Urge respondents to think specifically of the person they work for when completing the exercise. The directions are simple. If they *Strongly Agree* with the statement, write the number *4* in the box following it. If they *Agree* with the statement, write the number *2*. If they *Strongly Disagree* with the statement, write the number *1*.

- My view of compensation is consistent with the organization's compensation policies. □
- The organization supports the way I approach my subordinates. □
- My subordinates understand my influence with the decision-making hierarchy of the organization. □
- Top management creates an environment in which people motivate and direct themselves toward a common goal. □
- My subordinates are rewarded for independent thought. □
- My manager communicates an interest in my career. □
- Top management has the best interests of its employees in mind. □
- My suggestions and ideas are heard by top management. □
- My organization has clearly defined its corporate goals and business objectives. □
- Top management shares information about its business philosophy. □

Here's how to evaluate the results. If a score falls:

Between 10–20:   The Trust Quotient on this factor is *low.* Respondents feel isolated from top management.

Between 21–25:   The Trust Quotient is *a little below average.* They feel somewhat removed from top management and would like to feel supported more consistently.

Between 26–34: The Trust Quotient is *somewhat above average.* Respondents feel that there is adequate communication with top management and that opportunities are available to gain some support for their views.

Between 35–40: The Trust Quotient is *very high.* Respondents feel that his/her views and those of subordinates are supported by top management, and that lines of communication are open.

Similar tests can be developed for employees at any level of the organization.

C. Once you've got the results of this exercise in hand, determine whether there's a gap between individual and organization perceptions in four key areas: Values, Expectations, Interests, and Success. Place check marks (√) in areas of agreement in the matrix provided:

	Organization	*Individual*
Values		
Trust		
Interests		
Success		

If the check marks don't indicate agreement, then individuals and the organization are not in agreement. Don't panic if you don't have a total consensus. Complete agreement is almost impossible. The real danger is when *none* of these issues are in alignment. (Conversely, if you find the matrix filled with double check marks in each area, then the problem may not be as serious as you suspect.)

One of our clients—a telecommunications company— tried this exercise recently, and the results show that individual values, trust, interests, and definitions of success were terribly out of whack. The organization, for example, defined success, (in part), as providing the best long-distance service to its customers. Most employees—through no fault of their own—didn't place a high value on customer service. They saw their success in terms of their own departmental goals or the goals of their own particular programs. This is common in organizations that are highly political in nature. Values have given way to turf protection, ego massaging, and personal agendas. These kinds of environments are very difficult to change because those who thrive in them have less to lose (and everything to gain) if the status quo remains the same.

Alignment is the great acid test of analysis. When you see a dramatic imbalance in values, one thing should become clear: it will be very difficult—if not impossible—for the organization to move forward as it exists now.

Let's assume that personal and organizational values are, in fact, out of alignment in your company. Where do you go from here?

Step 2: Cut to the Chase: Define Success

In most cases, success—and how people perceive it—lies at the core of a values crisis. So we have to go to the heart of the problem to tackle the larger issues. Think back to the early part of the book when we went through this exercise on an individual level. After we examined what was important to us as individuals (and perhaps concluded that all was not right with our own values), the next step was to fashion our own definition of success. The same holds true at an organizational level. Up to this point, virtually all of our definitional work has been aimed at helping you gauge your own feelings toward success as well as determining whether individual and organizational definitions are out of alignment. Now it's time to nail it down and go directly to the source—the people around you. A clear understanding of what will make the entire organization successful must be established before we can reshape values. Defining success begs the question—"What will make our company or organization more like success is for me?" (In chapter Four we discussed the basics of success, now comes the hard part—applying it directly to your organization.)

Let's first look at the traditional definitions of success that haven't worked:

• *Companies have long defined success in terms of the bottom line.* Making x percent over plan," "upping sales by x percent" or "growing market share by x percent" are common. Fair enough. But let's think about this for a minute. Is a percentage gain in profits or sales really a good indicator of success? Wall Street, which tends to think in short-term, bottom-line results, might think so. But how many businesses are in it only for the short term? How many employees are in for one or two quarters? And will your customers continue to do business with you because you'll keep them happy for three to six months? Hardly. When companies focus solely on the bottom line, it's like saying, "One good meal will keep me very happy." Short-term results won't give you inner happiness. They won't make employees happy. And they sure won't keep customers satisfied for very long.

• *Companies exist to enhance shareholder value.* How many times have we heard this one? Naturally, a rising stock price is going to keep investors happy. But it leaves out employees—the very people that you have to depend on to increase stock value—long after the stock market's infatuation wanes. And it certainly doesn't leave much room for customers.

• *Companies exist to build great products.* True, but you need more than great products. Pierce Arrow made a truly great car at one time; they are no longer in business. So too did LaSalle and Tucker and a host of other car companies. Pan Am was a great, airline—its service was unsurpassed. But it didn't survive either.

It's no coincidence that many of these organizations also suffered from protracted battles with organized labor before they disappeared.

What's missing in each one of these cases? It's almost always the same—employees and customers. It's a vicious circle. When the needs and concerns of employees are left out of the picture, it's a good bet that eventually service goes right out the door, and customers are left out in the cold as well. If employees don't feel successful—if their desires and hopes aren't being fulfilled—do you think they're really going to be concerned about the needs of customers?

I think traditional, bottom-line oriented definitions of success never worked well to begin with. Given today's world, they're even more useless as important goals. For most people success goes beyond take-home pay. People feel that they are most successful when they are contributing to an effort. They equate success with inner peace or fulfillment. So we have to expand our definition of success in order to include those who have been excluded for too long, and by acknowledging that personal fulfillment *is* critical to success. General Electric has done a marvelous job of recognizing this issue. In fact, GE Chairman Jack Welch says, "General Electric does not only exist for shareholder investment. But for the fulfillment of employees." Notice that he doesn't define fulfillment. He leaves that up to the employees. And so should you.

Put together a team of employees—preferably a cross-section of your work force—then select a point person to head the group, and ask them to find out how employees truly define success. I should note here that this exercise takes perceptions of success to a deeper level than the one we completed in chapter six. Develop a questionnaire for all employees, posing several questions on the issue. Make sure the survey doesn't focus solely on success, but on the factors that make people feel successful. Here's a sample question-naire:

1. What makes you feel successful?
2. I would feel more successful if I were allowed to:

_____

_____

_____

3. What makes you feel fulfilled?
4. Do you feel fulfilled by your job now? If not, why?
5. How does your department/organization view success?

6. If it was up to you, how would you define success for your department/organization?
7. Do you understand what's expected of you on the job?
8. Are your expectations in sync with those of the company, your boss, and your peers?
9. Do you feel as if you are making a real contribution?

Compile and analyze the results. The answers should further clarify the positions from our initial survey earlier in the chapter. You may find—as we have in the past—that the way people perceive success, both for themselves and their organizations, are dramatically different than what is commonly accepted as success. When we've put this question to client employees, there's never been a shortage of answers. Here are a few examples that are typical of what we've found:

"I'd feel successful if I thought I was being appreciated for my day-to-day contributions and my skills, not the relationship I have with the boss."

"I want to go home at night knowing that the quality of my work is appreciated and valued."

"I want to be judged by how I perform, not who I'm friends with."

"I would feel fulfilled if I knew that what I did was really going to help humanity."

"I would feel better about what I do if I could see how it all ties together."

Notice that money is not mentioned in *any* of the above quotes. We rarely see it in definitions of success. The bottom line is that how a company arrives at a definition of success is as important as the definition itself. What good is a company's definition if it does not reflect the views of the people *whose responsibility it is to make the company successful?* When a company doesn't take the time to ask employees, and when employees don't contribute to the definition, the result is a wooden, artificial concept that looks good on the front cover of an annual report but has absolutely no meaning.

So how do we go about the actual process of defining success for your organization? Let's look at the qualities of a possible definition. There are no hard and fast rules to this process. In fact, when it's done right, each definition of success is as individual as the company it comes from because it takes everyone in the organization into consideration. It is not a 10,000-word tome that is written and rewritten until everything that is understandable is wiped out of it. A good definition strikes a balance. It says simply and succinctly that the organization will:

- Perform well.
- Balance cost controls, sales, and quality.
- Contribute to the well-being of society and to each individual in the organization.
- Provide balanced lifestyles for employees, whereby people can manage their own careers, fulfill the expectations of their families, and enable them to contribute to the well-being of society.
- Generally service customers.

Going It Alone

I've said it before, but it's worth repeating here: Redefining success is a task that should not be done alone. Now it's time to put together a team consisting of a cross-section of employees representing each region or department, or both. Appoint someone in-house to lead the effort. Use an outside consultant. Encourage each participant to share their results among their colleagues and invite as much comment as possible. This should be an organization-wide effort. Once an initial draft has been completed, it should go back to each individual for review. Comments should be invited, and when possible, incorporated into the final draft. It's also important to stress that no definition is ever final. A good one should change with the organization, reflecting the most current needs and demands.

Step 3: Develop a Mission Statement

Once you define success, the next step is to create a mission statement. Mission statements have historically served as corporate bibles—blueprints that define an organization's purpose, its reason for being, and the characteristics that will make it successful. A good mission statement should be an outgrowth of the organization's view of success. It says in very short order, "Who we are, what we do and for whom." The best mission statements come from the heart—bring employees into the process. Ask them to:

- Write their own personal mission statement.
- Detail the action steps that must be completed to accomplish their mission.
- Discuss the obstacles that might prevent them from completing their mission.
- Determine how those obstacles can be overcome.

- Develop their own concept of a mission statement for your organization.

Molding a Mission Statement

Most mission statements are written by a senior executive or a well-intentioned public relations person who knows how to put a good spin on words. There's nothing wrong with clarity. The trouble is: Few companies give much thought to the issues that really make them successful before putting the words down on paper. The sad truth is that most mission statements *aren't real,* because they aren't aligned with the way employees define success. Mission statements must be a partnership between an organization and its people. Here's a good example of a national mission that had little support from Americans: The nationwide 55 mile per hour speed limit. When it was imposed in 1973, the mission was to save lives and cut fuel consumption. Those are pretty important goals. But few bought into it. Not many drivers slowed down. Fuel consumption dipped, but not for long. Today, many states have abandoned the 55 m.p.h. limit altogether—a testament to what happens when there's no consensus. Likewise, when a mission statement becomes less than a partnership, and one side stipulates all the conditions, you wind up with companies that are racing around without much consideration for where they're going. The point is do not develop your mission statement in a vacuum. A team approach, headed by empowered leaders, is the right way to begin.

Here's a "before-and-after" snapshot of mission statements from Consolidated Natural Gas:

[Original]

CNG's Producing Company's Mission is to be an efficient finder, producer, and premium marketer of oil and gas. The successful accomplishment of this mission will result in a better-than-market competitive return and significant growth value for CNG shareholders. We want to be among the leading independent producers, if not the leader. We want it to be known that what we do, we do very well.

CNGP recognizes the importance of System teamwork and will cooperate with its affiliate companies to maximize the competitive advantage of the System . . . CNG Producing will focus its activities in basins and markets where it can be most profitable. We will appropriately balance our efforts in oil and gas exploration, development, and acquisitions both offshore and onshore . . . We will seek strong partners who will help us achieve our objectives, and we theirs. Our objective will be to build strategic alliances that encompass all functions.

Employees will be kept fully advised of the strategies, plans and goals so they know the Company's direction and their own critical importance to the Company's future success . . .

What do you think of this mission statement? Take a moment to evaluate this example using the following chart:

Length:	Too short ☐	Too long ☐	Just right ☐
Content:	Vague ☐	Too specific ☐	Adequate ☐
Focus:	Employee ☐	Management ☐	Customer ☐

What's wrong with this example? We feel it's too long. (We've provided only excerpts.) It focuses too heavily on strategy, and not enough on the human element of the business. It does not acknowledge employees as valuable contributors, nor does it reflect their views on success and goals. It talks a lot about *what* the business does, but it really doesn't address *how* the organization does business.

Look at the difference when CNG went back to the drawing board and devised a new mission statement after a careful analysis of success factors and values, coupled with the proper input from employees:

[*Revised*]

We are dedicated to becoming the premier exploration and production company. This means our single most important mission is to find and produce oil and gas reserves at a competitive cost and to sell them at the optimum profit margin. But it also means a commitment to provide our customers with a reliable source of supply and CNG's shareholders with a superior overall return on investment. We recognize this mission will only be accomplished through the efforts of our employees, and therefore we have an obligation to make CNGP an exciting, fulfilling place to work—a place where teamwork, innovation, and risk taking are valued and rewarded.

What's right with this mission statement?

- It strikes a balance between success and values.
- It reflects the views of employees. In fact, it's in sync with employee values because employees played a big part in its development.
- The needs of the business, customers, key constituents,

and shareholders are all taken into consideration, and given equal importance.

- It tells everyone—even those who may know nothing about the company and what it does—exactly how the company goes about its business.

What are the elements of a well-thought out, dynamic mission statement? Again, mission statements are meant to be as individual as fingerprints. But there are common elements that characterize the best ones. Useful mission statements do the following:

- They focus on how a company "gets there."
- They tell what a company is all about today—the organization and its employees—and what they have to do to get there.
- They state—clearly and succinctly—how everyone in the organization defines success.
- They strike a balance among the company's goals, what its people believe in, the customers it serves, and the way it achieves success.

Finally, a good mission statement says something about how you do business. It says, "We're going to be cost conscious, sales conscious, quality conscious, sensitive to each other, and we're going to define the focus of the firm as:

- "Commitment to the customer"
- "Commitment to employees"
- "Commitment to shareholders"
- "Commitment to society"

All four constituencies are elevated to an equal plane. No one overshadows the other. No group suffers at the expense of another. That's the way it ought to be—balanced.

Now, before I continue, it's important to point out that one of the big reasons why Consolidated Natural Gas has such a remarkable mission statement is because senior management had the foresight to make it happen. And that's a key point that I can't underscore enough. Without support from the top, no re-evaluation program—no matter how well conceived or executed—will work. Another major success factor is that the mission statement was developed by a team that represented the entire organization. The document was reviewed and commented on by everyone in the company. There were numerous drafts. But by the time it was finished, it had the backing (and the confidence) of the entire organization. People felt they had a stake in the document. Consensus building is critical at every phase of the values building process. Without it, you're back on the freeway, and no one's doing 55 whether you want them to or not!

Step 4: Developing a Vision

Does a company need a *vision?* Would you attempt a cross-country journey without a road map? Make no mistake, a vision is important. It describes the future image of the organization. It focuses on the future. Often, it's a wish list of where the company wants to be, and it's rooted in credible and realistic terms, whereas a mission statement focuses more on today. A vision *also* must come from the top of the organization. Do not underestimate the importance of a vision. Shortly after he took over the helm of IBM, CEO Louis Gerstner was harshly criticized for not having a vision for the company. Competitors like Compaq Computer jumped all over this and used it as a leveraging point to lure potential customers. Analysts and the computer trade press began questioning Gerstner's abilities. Within a matter of months, Gerstner came back with a vision for the company.

Likewise, when a new President takes office, the first thing everyone looks for in his initial State of the Union Address is his vision for America. A vision statement doesn't have to come only from the head of the organization. It should also reflect the views of employees and important constituencies served by the organization. It can be developed by a group or task force within the company and later endorsed by the CEO. It can be offered by the CEO with a challenge to the company to develop a more permanent statement. It should not—under any circumstances—be imposed from the top. Whatever the case, it's important that senior management endorse the statement and communicate that commitment throughout the company.

What constitutes a great vision statement?

It must take employees into account. Or else as Edwin A. Locke, in *The Essence of Leadership,* sums it up: "Sometimes top management sees an apple. When it gets to middle management, it's an orange. By the time it gets to us, it's a lemon."

The best way to ensure that your vision statement will have meaning to employees is to solicit their advice. At this point, it would be appropriate to survey focus groups or representatives who are participating in the values redevelopment process. Ask the following:

- Does the company have a vision?
- If so, what is this vision?
- Do you agree with this vision?
- Describe your vision for the future of the company.

As with the other categories of questions, you'll be amazed with the responses. Consider them carefully and incorporate those that make the most sense into a draft that should be reviewed and commented on by representatives from all your offices.

What else should a good vision statement include? Here's a checklist:

- A vision statement should reflect the culture and values of your organization.
- It should reflect the desires of employees, customers, important constituencies, and, if publicly owned, the share-owners.
- A vision statement should take into account all obstacles—internal and external—facing the company.
- As with all aspects of values rebuilding, the vision statement should be communicated to everyone that's affected by it.

Finally, the vision statement should be bold and imaginative. It should set goals. For example, if your organization is the number three windshield wiper manufacturer in the country, and your goal is to become number one in sales and customer satisfaction by the end of the century, then your vision should say so. Perhaps no vision was more compelling than the one that President John F. Kennedy set for NASA in

1963—"to land a man on the moon before this decade is out and return him safely to earth."

- Vision statements need to be updated. What was right for 1972 may, in fact, be completely off the mark today. And don't chisel a vision statement in stone. It will quickly become outdated and useless. Make it flexible and revisit it whenever the organization sees fit.

Step 5: Developing a Values Code

The vision statement reaches out into the future. The mission statement is a great high-level, strategic tool. But for everyday practice, we need to bring that vision down to ground floor level—to something that everyone in the organization can relate to and use. Our next step then is to develop a very precise *values code* (or as some companies prefer, a "code of ethics") that spells out exactly how to deal with real-life business situations. Much of the legwork for this process has been done already from our work prior to developing a mission statement. So far, we analyzed and redefined the organization's definition of success; we've extensively surveyed employees about values, trust, and fulfillment; and our new mission statement serves as a guide.

Writing a values code is an enormously challenging project because it requires someone who can interpret a ton of information and boil it down into a cohesive set of guidelines that are easy to understand and follow. It is for this very reason that I recommend that this be left to an individual who has played a major role in the mission statement effort—possibly a team leader, an organizational psychologist who understands the issues involved, or maybe someone who has participated in the effort but hasn't had an up-front role. I'm not saying that this step should be done by one or two people in a closet. Quite the contrary. You will need buy-in across the organization once again for a values code to work. What you don't need at this stage of the project is a committee to write all the rules. You need somebody who's got the foresight and understanding of the situation to compress all the facts, develop the document, and shepherd it through the approvals. Let the committee approve or disapprove, but have one or two people have to do the drafting, much like Thomas Jefferson drafted the *Declaration of Independence.*

AT&T has developed an excellent values code that serves as a fitting example:

Our Common Bond

We commit to these values to guide our decisions and behavior:

Respect for Individuals

We treat each with respect and dignity, valuing individual and cultural differences. We communicate frequently and with candor, listening to each other regardless of level or position. Recognizing that exceptional quality begins with people, we give individuals the authority to use their capabilities to the fullest to satisfy the customers. Our environment supports personal growth and continuous learning for all AT&T people.

Dedication to Helping Customers

We truly care for each customer. We build enduring relationships by understanding and anticipating our customers' needs and by serving them better each time than the time before. AT&T customers can count on us to consistently deliver superior products and services that help them achieve their personal or business goals.

Highest Standards of Integrity

We are honest and ethical in all our business dealings, starting with how we treat each other. We keep our promises and admit our mistakes. Our personal conduct ensures that AT&T's name is always worthy of trust.

Innovation

We believe innovation is the engine that will keep us vital and growing. Our culture embraces creativity, seeks different perspectives and risks pursuing new opportunities. We create and rapidly convert technology into products and services, constantly searching for new ways to make technology more useful to customers.

Teamwork

We encourage and reward both individual and team achievements. We freely join with colleagues across organizational boundaries to advance the interests of customers and shareowners. Our team spirit extends to being responsible and caring partners in the communities where we live and work.

> By having these values AT&T aspires to set a standard of excellence worldwide that will reward our shareowners, our customers and all AT&T.

The last paragraph is really important because it reinforces the company's three primary constituencies—in this case, shareowners, customers, and employees—and it says they are all on the same level. Is this the right values code for every organization? No, but it's right for this particular organization, because it is tailored to address the needs and goals of the people of AT&T. The specifics of your particular situation should dictate the tone and tenor of your organization's value code. But here's a list of common elements that should characterize a workable values code:

- *Keep it simple.* Stay away from jargon. Resist cliches. Avoid corporate doublespeak. Get to the point. These are codes. If people have to go through the trouble of figuring them out, acceptance will be low.
- *Don't be preachy.* Remember, the shared values process is a partnership. If you talk *down* to your partners they will quickly pick up on it, and they'll resent it. Much of what you're trying to accomplish will be undone in a very short time.
- *Avoid personal singular personal pronouns. I, me,* and *yours,* are poor substitutes for *ours,* and *we.*
- *Make sure the codes are current.* They should reflect the realities and viewpoints of today—not 30 years ago. If, for example, entertaining is a big part of your business then you should take the trouble to define what is acceptable— and what isn't—in terms of giving gifts to clients, offering

tickets to entertainment events, or holding dinner meetings. Ethical issues for corporations are often influenced by law. And since the laws change frequently, it's best to update your value code whenever it seems appropriate. Some organizations re-examine their entire values program every few years.

Step 6: Implementing the Program

So far, we've attempted to define success, develop a mission statement, and establish a values code. (Depending on the size of the organization this process could take up to a year or more.) What's next? *Implementation,* or what we call, *direction.* We must now make our Pinocchio real—part of the fabric of the way the organization does business. Here's where the potential for danger is the greatest. If all this work isn't presented properly, and in a way that will encourage people to stand up and notice, you'll wind up with an expensive dust collection on your hands. Direction is an eight-step process that cuts to the heart and soul of your organization. Don't assume that some of these steps can be cut out or circumvented. Think of each one as a step on a staircase. You need each one to get to the top. The seven steps to direction are:

1. *Communicate.* None of these documents will do you a bit of good if they sit in an operating manual. You've got to get the word out. Prepare each document carefully—making sure there are no mistakes. Put them together in a Values and/ or Mission Kit, and see to it that every single employee gets a copy. The kit should include a letter or a videotaped message from the head of the company or from one of the leaders in the shared values effort. Nothing beats word of mouth.

Managers should be personally briefed on the values program, and they in turn, should be asked to brief the people who report to them. It's important to walk people through the entire packet. This ensures that people are familiar with the program and know who to get answers from. Remember, this must be perceived by the entire organization as "our" program; not another instrument of top management. Senior management should back the program. They shouldn't act like they own it.

2. *Share the values program with suppliers and customers.* Sharing means more than just sending a copy of the program to your key mailing list. You should, when possible, develop a values-to-values shared marketing program with suppliers and customers. For suppliers, it sends a signal about how you do business and that you expect others to play at the same level if they expect to continue as your suppliers. For customers, a shared values program serves two purposes—first, it demonstrates your commitment to serving their needs, and second, it acts as an educational tool that will help them—if they so choose—to develop their own values program. When the organization and its customers share similar values programs, the bond between both sides is enhanced. Common goals become easier to achieve, and, ultimately, both sides end up with healthier relationships.

3. *Base appraisals on values.* Every performance appraisal should be based on the values program of the company. Values need to be discussed during every performance appraisal. This has to be more than just, "Jenny has high values." Managers should judge employees not only in terms of how well they do their jobs, but by how well they uphold the values of the company. Setting the groundwork begins long before the appraisal itself—values should be read and reviewed at every major management meeting, as they pertain to that meeting.

4. *Review company programs and base meetings on your values code.* Every program should be based on the company's values program. This includes quality and training programs and other programs that affect employee morale and development. The effectiveness of meetings should also be reviewed against the values code. This can be done by simply asking people, "Do you feel we are being honest or clear on this subject?"

5. *Benchmark.* Annual reviews should be held with all constituents—customers, employees, and shareholders—to ensure that the company is living up to its values code in the eyes of the people it serves. People who know and depend on the organization have a keen sense—they're quick to pick up on changes—and they'll let you know immediately whether or not they're seeing a difference. Some companies might want to take this process a step further by asking someone in the organization to coordinate this effort. You may want to ask your in-house public relations experts to help. Many are familiar with surveys and issues assessment. Public relations organizations—like the Public Relations Society of America and the International Association of Business Communicators—do this sort of self-assessment all the time. Often, it consists of extensive surveys or focus groups of key constituents, followed by an extensive analysis. You may want to contact a chapter of one of these organizations in your community for advice, or if you have public relations professionals in your organization, look to them for guidance and assistance.

6. *Create a diffused power base.* In a values-based organization, traditional power structures cease to exist. Why? Traditional structures lock people into boxes which condition employees to think in very narrow terms—"This is your job, this is my job, and that's as far as I'll go."

TRADITIONAL ORGANIZATIONAL CHART

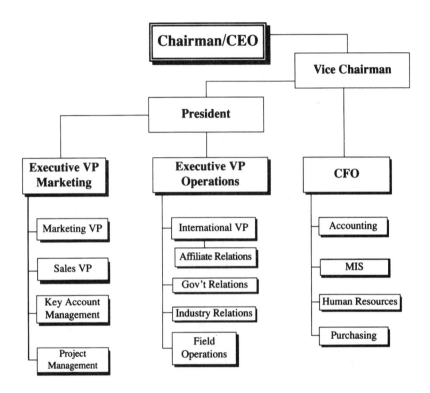

The lines between the boxes create distances between people. In most corporations, we talk about "what we do," not "how we can serve." Lost in the shuffle is the customer—nobody thinks about the customer on the receiving end. And job descriptions rarely tell employees what they have to do to make the business more successful. Values programs are designed to get everyone in the organization thinking about what they can do to serve, to contribute and to be of value. In a values system, the power base must be redefined. You will still have levels of responsibility, supervisors, and employees. But *everyone* must share equally in the responsibility for values.

How does this new organization differ from the past? To begin with, the new organization has an acceptable code of behavior that defines how the company will do business. And second, all constituents are treated equally. What this does is sensitize the entire company to two things—service and balance. Think about what this means. Employees are treated just as if they were the company's biggest shareholders.

If you are an accountant, your role is just as important as that of the salespeople. The needs of every customer—no matter how big or small—are treated with equal importance. Here's how the old organizational structure has been reordered to reflect the new commitment to values:

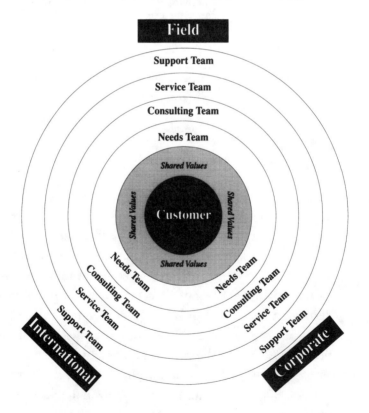

7. *Keep the values system alive.* Establishing a values base is only half the challenge—keeping these values alive and meaningful for the future is the other half. It's important to reiterate here that values are a long-term commitment. They can't be written, hung on the wall, and left there to collect dust. An organization must maintain a constant vigilance over its values base to ensure that it is meaningful for the times, the issues, and the people it covers. This is a real balancing act—the organization must find new ways to keep the mission fresh, define success, and to keep sales, cost controls, and quality properly aligned. The way to do this is through vigorous benchmarking, an active review program, continuous feedback from employees, and an ongoing commitment from senior management.

Step 7: Establishing an Organizational Watchdog

Some companies like the idea of an omnibusperson program to ensure proper adherence to values. But these are often one-person jobs that focus more on the problem than the cure. The challenge today demands a more proactive approach—building an organizational structure that lives and breathes around the people that the organization serves.

Ensuring Success

How can you guarantee that values will not end up in the corporate scrap heap of programs and slogans of the month? Once a fully-functioning values program like the one described here is put in place, it's difficult for an organization to go back to the way it was. You can't go halfway out on a limb with a true values program and then slam the door on it. The organization won't let it happen. If an organization takes all the right steps to institute a values program, this is what should happen:

- Power bases should cease to be as important.
- Adding unnecessary staff (pyramiding)—particularly during good times—will lessen.
- Employees will start thinking on behalf of the company and customers—cost-consciousness becomes second nature. Service improves.
- Open communications will occur more readily.
- Service to the customer will become more important than lines of authority and accountability.
- People will stop thinking in terms of "me" vs. "them."
- Employee attitudes will start to improve. People will become more helpful rather than territorial.
- People won't talk so much about money. They won't be preoccupied with making sales quotas and salary levels. Bottom-line results will become points of measurement rather than of short-term condemnation.
- Employees will start talking about service, camaraderie, caring, their communities, education, skills development, the future, and personal contributions rather than the direction of the firm.
- The people in your organization will look forward to the future with greater confidence.

Case Studies: How Do We Know it Will Work?

How can we be so sure of the benefits of values rebuilding? Where's the proof to back up the premise that shared values will do everything we say it will *and* improve business? We know that values re-engineering has worked at companies like Motorola and Johnson & Johnson, among others. But the whole notion of rebuilding values is still so new—and untested—that there's no escaping the fact that much of the evidence is anecdotal. What *we do know* is that our current course of action is not working. We also have a wealth of surveys and statistics showing that downsizings and restructurings are not helping, but hurting us. As I've mentioned before, given both time and experience, I believe we'll see the kind of evidence that proves the need for values in today's business world. I'd like to relay two examples that best illustrate how companies have benefited from a new shared values systems. The first is Boatmen's First National Bank in Kansas City, a long-time DBM client. The second one might surprise you—DBM itself.

Case Study I: Boatmen's First National Bank

Following a major restructuring that included shared values, boatmen's has seen a drop in employee turnover, an increase in productivity, and a higher return on assets. Here's their story:

Boatmen's had to lay off employees in 1989 after acquiring Centerre Bancorp of Kansas City. Having already experienced a host of productivity and morale problems during a

1985 merger, the bank asked DBM to guide the two organizations through the transition.

The company took great pains to ensure that the layoffs would not disproportionately affect certain demographic groups, such as minorities or older employees. Managers were trained to prepare them to implement the layoffs, which soon followed. After the layoffs the bank strived to keep the remaining employees well informed about their plans. The company restructured its entire values system and implemented a new mission statement and values code. Since then, turnover at Boatmen's dropped from 28 percent annually to 14.7 percent. The drop in turnover saved the bank hundreds of thousands of dollars in recruiting and training costs, and helped boost productivity. Also, the bank's return on assets has grown from .33 percent to .95 percent.

Can we say for certain that a stronger values system is responsible for the good news at Boatman? Not for certain. But we can say—with a high degree of certainty—that the debilitating effects of Silent Sabotage were averted and actually reversed because the organization met them head-on in a proactive manner. That's something to be said about values.

Case Study II: Drake Beam Morin

Because my experience with DBM is first hand, I can give you a first-hand account of what it's like to go through the values rebuilding process. DBM has served as a test model for much of what you have been reading. Our program has been in place since 1991, and although implementation is not yet complete, our experience illustrates the good things that can happen when an organization focuses on values and makes a systematic effort to rebuild them.

I am frankly amazed at the difference our efforts have made in the tenor and quality of our organization. And it is in this spirit that I present our story.

Step 1: Recognizing the Problem

Let's turn the clock back to 1991. At the time, we were already the leading human resources management company in our field and we had a world renowned reputation. Our business with corporate clients was growing at a tremendous rate—20 to 25 percent a year annual since 1968. But behind the scenes DBM was becoming known as a slick, insensitive, get-it-done company. We were known for doing good work, but we were not known for great quality. At the same time, as more and more companies began re-examining their human resources needs, fast-moving competitors were making inroads into our business. Individuals who had been laid off by client companies and then sent to us for counseling regarded our program as something of a grist-mill; a cookie-cutter factory for those trying to rebuild their careers.

Internally, our own DBM job trainees felt they were going through a mindless process, not an individualized experience that would help them in their specific roles. Regular employees were becoming disenchanted. They felt no one cared about them, and generally expected to do the bidding of management and get on with it. Surveys of our employees indicated that:

- Internally, communications was inadequate.
- We did a poor job of talking to each other and sharing information.
- We were becoming more concerned about returns

than service. There was a lot of "me/them" terminology in our language.
- Customers said we weren't returning phone calls as rapidly as we should.
- There was a general erosion in caring about clients and colleagues within the organization and it was becoming obvious to the people who depended on us.

As CEO, I sensed that there was a problem, but I didn't know the extent of what was going on. Looking back, it was easy to overlook our shortcomings—we were in an industry that was growing by leaps and bounds. And among our peers, we were still the leading firm of our kind in the world. Our reputation—while not sterling—was still solid. And we had a mission statement and a code of ethics hanging on the wall. I wrote them. Overall, I felt we had a lot to be proud of. But then one evening, when a client asked for help in redesigning his own organization's values program, I realized that DBM was also in trouble. It was the closest thing I've ever had to a corporate out-of-body experience. By objectively focusing on a client's problem, I could see that we had become much like that fellow in the Dun & Bradstreet ad— willing to do whatever it takes to get new business, even at the expense of caring and compassion. It also dawned on me that I was playing a major role in all of this. Suddenly, all the growth in numbers at DBM seemed meaningless. I felt a deep sense of frustration about myself and the direction of the entire DBM organization. I started checking with other members of management, and they too felt uneasy.

For myself, this awakening to the challenge was the first step in developing DBM's values program. I have since talked to senior executives from other companies who have had similar experiences. Often, it is little more than a feeling, an unsettling sensation that triggers a larger self-examination. For me, it took the experience of a client to see the problems within my own life and the organization. But it doesn't matter where or when it happens. The important thing is *to act* on the feeling, and not just let it slide, and to also be aware of the need to change.

What happened next?

There was no set plan at first. To begin with, I spent a lot of time thinking and re-examining and later rebuilding my own values, which was detailed in chapter one. From there, I knew that as a company, DBM had to go through the same kind of awakening—an intensive retrospective review that would help us gain a better understanding of ourselves, what we do, and who we serve. I felt that in order to get where we needed to be that we had to find out what makes us tick—how we defined success and values—and balance those factors in a way that would allow everyone in the organization to achieve a greater sense of fulfillment. As the head of the company, I felt that I had to become a driving force in this process. It was up to me to start the process and communicate it in a way that everyone would understand and become excited about. I also knew that none of this could happen without a vision—a sense of direction that was believable, obtainable, rational, and had infinite possibilities. Without it, we'd continue to muddle along as a rudderless organization. That meant that I had to become to the best of my ability—a visionary.

In short, it was clearly up to me to provide a vision of where the organization was heading *and* to be a catalyst for change. So I spent a great deal of time asking myself, "What kind of company should DBM be?" I also began seeking outside counsel about how best to accomplish this task.

For example, we had to go from a company based on outplacement consulting to an organization seeking many paradigms for meeting new needs; we had to become human resources partners to our clients, we had to progress from a company that simply takes client orders to a company that assesses client needs and solves problems. Finally, we had to become a highly motivated company that works in teams and a global company, driven not by self-interest but by a customer/team driven approach.

To get there, I asked myself and others around me, what kind of environment would we need to achieve this? The answers—which eventually formed my vision for the company—centered on the human element of our organization. It appeared that we needed an environment that would do the following:

- Evaluate people not on the basis of sales records, but in terms of satisfied customers and how "we treat each other."
- Recognize people who offer ideas.
- Judge employees by actions rather than by their political skills.
- Balanced the rate of growth.
- Embrace change as a friend rather than an enemy.
- Depend on the value of each individual's skills and team efforts.
- Be based solidly on values.

Then, given these considerations, I asked myself, "What would be my vision of the company success?" These answers came back. The company would:

- Be a place for stimulating, productive, and creative work.
- Alignment with colleagues of a very similar work ethic.
- Provide a commitment to excellence as a shared

value, and defined by the organization in a way that is acceptable to all.

- Give everyone a sense of involvement in and control over our collective and individual destinies.
- Offer psychological and financial rewards for both collective and individual contributions.
- Provide an opportunity to experience spiritual and educational growth as a professions and as part of a team.
- Include an atmosphere of mutual professional respect.
- Give everyone a clear sense of the direction, values, and professional ethics of the organization.

Shortly after this, we had our annual employee conference in Tucson, Arizona. I stood before the entire staff on a plainly lit stage and challenged everyone to build a new company on a foundation of redefined values. Looking back, I didn't know exactly how this would happen, but I knew we had to change both in terms of purpose and abilities. I also knew that this wouldn't work if it were imposed from the top by me. DBM's change had to come from the bottom up, with the help of every employee. And before anything could really happen, our organization had to define success, develop a new mission, and uncover the values that our organization held dear—in a way that everybody could live with.

So before I left the podium, I shared my thoughts, hopes, and aspirations for DBM. I said:

"DBM would become the kind of organization that any corporation or individual would feel privileged to work with. DBM must provide a service that is perceived as a profession . . . a place to work whereby you are evaluated by subordinates, peers, and management, because of the insightfulness of your ideas and actions rather than your political skills. DBM must be an environment where all people who offer 'ideas' are rewarded first for having the courage to offer the idea before it is ever reviewed.

Working for DBM is a totally human experience whereby we treat each other and our clients like we would like to be treated and we are evaluated not on a basis of more sales, but in terms of satisfied customers and candidates. DBM should be an organization that does not create dependency on the organization but rather on the value of each individual's skills. We never want professionals to feel stripped of their personal values and skills because of the corporate entity called DBM. And, finally, DBM must grow at a balanced rate."

I could tell from the reaction—a very quiet room—that few believed it was possible. People were suspicious. I couldn't blame them—my modus operandi at the time was watch the bottom line, get the job done, and each of you should feel lucky to be working here. So I was perceived as a slick, hard-driving guy that nobody messed around with. One fellow came up to me after the meeting and said, "I don't believe you. It's all lofty words." Other people didn't have the guts to say it, but I'd bet that more than two-thirds of DBM's employees didn't believe me either. To the disbelievers, all I could say was, "You don't have to like this, you don't have to agree with what I've said on this, but please give the process a chance." To their credit, most employees not only gave it a chance, they gave it much more. And the transformation that unfolded over the next two years was really quite remarkable.

Looking back, I think many felt for the first time that this was a chance to really make things happen.

Step Two: Defining the Mission and Values

Before the Tucson meeting was over, employees joined me in a series of case studies and exercises that examined how we responded to internal and external customers—colleagues and clients. What this did was get everyone thinking about their obligations to people, the state of their own personal ethics, and the state of their values.

We had about 500 professionals at the Tucson meeting. Throughout the Conference, they were split up into four groups of about 125 each. And together, we went through awareness exercises. One person in each group took notes on a flip chart of recommendations that came out of each meeting. There was no shortage of opinions, no lack of energy or enthusiasm. If anything, I'd say many of those who participated in the sessions felt as if they had been let out of a bottle. We had hundreds of suggestions. At the end of the day, a list was compiled of the values that were raised most often by these groups. Out of this came a starter list of shared values. These included attributes like honesty and integrity, respect for others, open communications, and teamwork. The list represented their value code, not mine.

While it marked a great beginning, this list only represented the views of our consultants and managerial staff. It didn't include clerical and certain administrative personnel. So we decided that everyone in the company worldwide should have a chance to reflect on the list and provide input. Together with Dr. Sandra Lanto, our organizational psychologist who was managing the project, we filmed a video tape informing employees about the project and the list of shared values which had been developed. We asked each of our seventy-five offices around the world to hold meetings, look at the list, and discuss what they felt were the shared values of their particular office team. From the start, we said that the meetings were completely voluntary. We told everyone to take off the gloves and do whatever you want—add their own values to the list, cross off those on the starter list that they didn't agree with, or change the existing ones. Confidentially was assured—to this day I still don't know who said what.

The only stipulation was that if they came up with their own values they had to define them in a way that everyone understood exactly what they were talking about. They were asked to send their suggestions back to us. And we gave ourselves a six-month deadline for completing this phase of the project.

The amazing thing is that during this initial round of input, we had 100 percent participation. Given the time-constraints of our business, it's rare to have this degree of consensus on anything. The overwhelming response probably stemmed from several factors:

- We struck a chord with people throughout the entire organization.
- Strong support from senior management.
- The hunger we all felt for something that brings a sense of purpose and meaning to our working lives.

There was a lot of advice too—most of it right on target. And the great majority of people wrote straight from the heart. Much of what we saw expressed concern over the rapid rate of change in the organization. Many felt that in this kind of environment it was important to keep some constants—something that they could hold onto—and that shared values were critical to that need for stability.

Most of the individual lists represented at least two hours of work at staff meetings. Many offices dedicated an entire day to the process. From this mountain of input, we developed a draft statement of shared values from the whole company. It focused on the values that we found most common among all the offices.

Along the way, we made a decision that if one office felt strongly about a specific suggestion that didn't show up our overall list, there was no reason why that office couldn't maintain it on their own. For example, there were some differences over issues such as humor. Some felt that sharing humor was a value in itself; part of the collegiality of the office. In a high-stress business, humor is important. But the issue wasn't shared company-wide, and that's why we opted for local rule. Similarly, there were differences in terms of what community outreach and involvement might mean. But we pressed ahead.

Once the draft statement was completed, it became the basis for further discussion. Here again, Dr. Lanto played a major role. She drafted and redrafted our documents for review throughout our various offices.

We asked everyone to focus on content only and ignore writing style. In hindsight, this proved impossible, as we soon discovered a whole world of budding DBM editors. Most offices put one person in charge of gathering input on the document and sending it back to headquarters. We asked that each office send back changes to Dr. Lanto. If there were no changes, they could send it back approved. If problems arose that couldn't be resolved at the office level, we invited each office to participate in a conference call with Dr. Lanto or another DBM professional to thrash things out. The whole process was designed to get buy-in of the document, and indeed, we found a consensus building as the project picked up steam. In fact, we could see a marked difference in attitudes from the beginning of the project—people wanted to make this thing work. In fact, in some offices where everyone wanted to be a part of the discussion, we had "telephone town meetings" involving dozens of employees at one time with multiple offices tied into the discussion. These were enormously helpful in building consensus because it made everyone in each of the offices feel as if they were a part of the entire process.

There were multiple rounds of telephone town meetings. For those offices that participated in earlier rounds, we promised that they would be contacted again if any of their key preferences were not consensual. When this happened in a few instances, the offices were pleasantly surprised at the phone call and expressed a willingness to live with the group consensus.

After this, a final draft of the mission and shared values statement was prepared, reflecting all of the input from the field. The final statement was prepared just before New Year's 1993. A copy was sent home to all employees within the United States, and to offices worldwide. Everyone in the organization was instructed to notify Sandra as soon as possible if there were any objections to the final draft. We held our collective breaths, but no serious objections were raised. So in January, 1993, a vote to approve the final draft was taken via a representative democracy at DBM's annual meeting. It's worth noting that one word change was proposed and approved at that meeting. The head of our European affiliate group added "worldwide" to our final draft. In today's global environment, it should have been second nature. The finished product, which hangs in every DBM office, looks like this:

DBM Worldwide Mission and Shared Values

DBM Mission

We are devoted to providing the finest quality organizational and individual transition consulting services, meeting and exceeding the requirements of those we serve. Our goal is to continue our industry leadership, adding value for our customers, colleagues, business partners and shareholders through consistent pursuit of excellence and commitment to our shared values.

DBM Shared Values

We share the following values as colleagues, striving constantly to translate these values into our work with our customers, colleagues and communities.

- Honesty and Integrity. We stand by our word, consistently and rigorously following through on all commitments.
- Respect for Others. We cherish diversity and respect each individual's need for a balanced life.
- Personal and Professional Excellence. We manage our individual careers and lives according to our highest personal and professional standards. We encourage challenge, risk-taking and lifelong learning as vital to creativity and excellence in all we do.
- Open Communications. We speak our hearts and minds and share information on a timely basis to build trusting,

productive relationships. We listen with sensitivity to others' viewpoints, making every effort to hear—rather than judge—new ideas and approaches.
- Teamwork. We collaborate with each other and with those whom we serve to achieve common objectives. These partnerships maximize our contributions and add spirit, humor and perspective to our work.
- Corporate Citizenship. We resolve to be good corporate citizens—making a positive difference in the communities we serve around the world.

Step 3: The Values Team

Overall, DBM's values development experience tracked closely to the process outlined in chapter seven. The set-up stage, which focused on analysis and consensus building, probably took a year. That may seem like a long time to some, but when you are setting up a program that should last the lifetime of the organization, a year really isn't very long.

So finally we had a statement that defined what we were all about. The next challenge was putting it into practice. For us, it came down to how do we turn this statement into results at DBM? How do we ensure that we behave exactly as we say we will?

At about the same time we were taking the wrappings off our new mission and values statement, we started identifying the places where our behaviors—individually and organizationally—were not as consistent with our new values objectives as we wanted them to be.

So, at our annual meeting in 1993 we created and put in place a "Commitments Team." This group was comprised of representatives from each geographic region in the United States, around the world, and at every level of the organization. Our Central United States region, for example, was represented by a receptionist from that region. An executive vice president represented the Southeast region. Every geographic location was represented. This group was charged with identifying any gaps in offices between actual behavior and our values objectives. This is not a big-brother, policing organization. It is more like a barometer. It exists to gauge opinions and recommend ways to make improvements at a company-wide level.

Targeting Critical Issues

Each of the members worked with representatives in local offices across their region to identify issues that could be addressed at a local level, and then those which had to be resolved across the organization. Once these issues were clearly labeled, each member of the Commitment Team returned to New York to present his or her findings to our Executive Committee, which was responsible for keeping our program alive and well. Out of this, seven corporate wide issues were earmarked. These included:

- Providing better technical information systems support for our operations.
- Better communication about how to integrate our traditional outplacement business with new, nontraditional business that was changing the face of DBM.
- Being more aggressive in solving customer needs. Most felt that we weren't asking our customers the right kinds of questions.
- More professional development opportunities.

- A better system for recognizing performance and rewards.
- Many felt that we had to do a better job of communicating between offices.

What became clear from this is that we did not have big ethical infractions going on within our company. In fact, the Commitments Team found that most staff felt that our problems stemmed more from our rapid growth than from a sense that we had lost our ethics. That's the good news. The not-so-good news was that up to this point, we had no light to guide us between right and wrong; and as the gaps were illuminated, we had all the elements in place for a potential disaster. The list of gaps was shown to our executive committee—the top department executives from across the company. A point person was named in each area from the committee to oversee the problem. If there was a gap area that didn't have an owner from the committee, we had a task force in place to pick up the responsibility and see it through to a solution.

What emerged from this process had a profound effect on our organization. Systems and procedures began to change. A problem didn't have to be escalated all the way up the chain of command before it got any attention. It was identified and targeted for resolution, quickly and efficiently, by people at every level of the organization. Point people were given the responsibility to get the job done. When a gap had a profound bearing on budgetary concerns—as was the case with our information support systems—the solution had to be presented to the executive committee for review. We started to see immediate results—for example, professional development efforts were expanded. Our entire information systems structure has been examined by an MIS consultant, and as a result, a comprehensive five-year plan was developed to bring our technology capabilities in line with the growing needs of our business. We've put cross-functional teams in place to help us better integrate our outplacement and non-outplacement services. We're de-emphasizing individual office activity and setting objectives that involve many departments and offices. We're also training people to work better in teams. And finally, the firm has started work on an integrated strategic long-range plan encompassing the entire organization.

All of this is still a work in progress, and it will continue to be that way as long as Drake Beam Morin is in business. That's the way it should be—a values program is a living process that continuously updates itself to reflect current needs, trends, and issues. In its current form, it's right for today. Who knows whether it will be right for our business two or three years from now? Tom Peters suggests that "there ought to be a 'values sunset statute'—throw out a third of your values every five years, or burn the lot and start over every 10 years."[2] We agree that the process of reviewing and revitalizing a values program is essential.

Meanwhile, we're doing everything we can to make the mission and shared values statement a part of life at DBM. We focus on it in new hire orientation and training sessions. We talk about it at every major meeting. Our Commitments Team continues its mission. Periodic conference calls help keep the unit in touch, and on top of any emerging gap issues. The group makes regular reports to the executive committee. Progress reports are issued throughout the entire company, in memos, newsletters, and face-to-face meetings. Our values statement hangs on my wall and I talk about it at great length with anyone meeting with us.

Today, even though we are still in the early phases of

[2]Thomas J. Peters and Nancy K. Austin, *A Passion for Excellence,* Random House, New York.

this project, DBM is a much different company than it was just a few years ago. For example, in January, 1994, we had our annual management meeting. What used to happen at these meetings was that the people at the top of the organizational chart would make reports on the performance of the company, and sometimes we would have workshops on different subjects. It was very one-dimensional—two-way communication was negligible. At our meeting in Cleveland, however, people were completely engaged. There was a great deal of discussion about major issues surrounding the business. A report on compensation at DBM by a consulting firm drew a great deal of attention. And during the report, a representative from the Commitments Team was on hand to talk about the issues that were raised by DBM staff over compensation. This kind of information is shared throughout the company. Now the process by which compensation and bonuses are determined is being demystified.

Turnover, although not high by industry standards, declined by twenty percent between 1992 and 1993. That's a dramatic improvement. And in terms of performance, 1993 was our best year ever. While it's hard to draw a bottom line correlation between our performance and the values program, I truly believe that a renewed sense of spirit, cooperation, and vitality in our organization was responsible for our performance. On the whole, 1994 was a challenging year, but our values program brought us through with a sense of direction and progress not present before in our history.

Here's a brief summary of the steps used to develop and implement a shared values program at DBM:

1. Clarify organization leaders' project objectives and commitment levels.

2. Build a plan for creating a bottoms-up values statement and a plan for communicating it throughout the entire organization.

3. Implement the plan, announce the project, and create a mission and shared values statement.

4. Develop a plan for assessing the gaps between the values statement and the current norm. Identify a team to oversee the identification and resolution of gaps.

5. Roll out the final statement to the staff. Celebrate and announce the oversight team for assessing gaps.

6. Implement a gap assessment program and communicate progress to the entire staff.

7. Working through the oversight team, analyze the results of the gap assessment, develop action recommendations, and propose them to organizational leaders.

8. Through the oversight team, announce the results of the gap assessment and the approved action recommendations to all staff.

9. Have the oversight team monitor progress on all actions and communicate progress to the entire staff on a regular basis.

10. Integrate the mission and shared values statement into all key external communications, staff development activities, and organizational events. Create appropriate vehicles for making the statement visible. Consider any proposed changes or updates annually.

Where does all of this end? It doesn't. A successful values program has to live and breathe and grow with the organization.

And when you see both the day-to-day and the long-term benefits of a values program in your own company, I'm willing to bet that you won't want it to end.

The Learning Process

What have we learned along the way?

• *Once you make a commitment to a values program, you can't turn back.* You will do more damage by telling people you're going to reengineer values and not following through, than by never attempting it at all. If we had stopped after the initial values statement was drafted, we might have had a mutiny on our hands. The process of reengineering values engages people. They make a personal commitment to its success. They feel betrayed when their work is shelved like a book. Once you put the ideals in writing, it becomes painfully obvious to everyone how far the organization has to move. Stop the motion and people have to live with that realization every single day.

• *Don't go it alone.* We were fortunate to have access to top-flight organizational professionals within our own organization who know the value of values, and how to go about reengineering them. I'm not saying this because DBM helps clients rebuild their values systems, but because I have seen first-hand what can happen when well-meaning executives put the wheels in motion, follow all the right guidelines, and stumble badly when they are hit by the unexpected. Values are intangible. Nothing about this process is guaranteed to go according to plan. When it works well, a values program will change your entire organization for the better. You have a lot riding on it. That's why it's worth seeking professional advice.

• *Expect change—and lots of it.* If you are not prepared to have the entire foundation of the company rocked by this process, don't do it.

• *Consensus is critical.* A bottoms-up approach won't work without buy-in. And while that may seem like a thorn in the early going, consensus building is the glue that will hold the program together later on.

• *Leadership from the top is also essential.* An activist approach by top management can make all the difference in the world. Without it, a bottoms-up approach will suffocate.

• *Set an example to follow.* Some of our clients are now seriously looking at our shared values program for their own organizations. We didn't go into this with the intention of marketing values, but we're finding that good values can be good business. When shared values spread, everyone wins. Client organizations become stronger, more efficient, and better workplaces. And these values can be a self-fulfilling prophecy. One program can lead to another. And all because someone put the ball in motion to begin with.

8

A Call for Values

"Values provide a common language for aligning a company's leadership and its people. A strategy is no good if people don't fundamentally believe in it."

ROBERT HAAS
CEO, LEVI STRAUSS & CO.

I had dinner with a friend who is in the throes of a values crisis. She's in sales and one day her boss walked into her office, threw her personal evaluation on her desk and said, "Here, read this." He then walked off and went into another meeting. As it turned out, the appraisal was very complimentary. There was only one sentence in the entire document that was negative, and of course, she focused on the negative. When she finally saw her boss, she got into a huge argument— not about her boss's inexcusable behavior at the appraisal— but about the one sentence. Now my friend is in the middle of a values crisis of her own. She's also wondering whether she should be looking for a job someplace else. Perhaps she should.

At another major firm that had a long-standing policy against layoffs, the edict came down from headquarters that the bar was being raised on performance appraisals. From now on, they said, it would be harder to score above average reviews. And by the way, the poorest performers would be fired. Managers were told to be tougher in grading employees on performance appraisals. So in comes a typical high performer for his annual review, fully expecting to be graded at least as well as a year ago, or maybe even higher. Instead, he's handed a downgrade, from "outstanding" to "meeting the requirements of the job." He walks out of the manager's office, bewildered and upset. And then at lunch, he learns that the grade was nothing personal. It was just his manager "towing the company line," so that it didn't look like he was handing out easy appraisals.

Neither of these two instances is isolated or atypical. If anything, I'd call them typical of what happens when values are sacrificed for the bottom line, and when profits take precedence over the human needs of doing business. Multiply these same two scenarios by a few thousand employees, and then again that by a few thousand employers, and you can imagine the kind of ripple effect that this type of behavior is having throughout our nation as a whole. Is it right? No. Is it the way things have to be? No. We can't let it happen, not if we expect to stay in business. There's too much at stake—too much riding on the outcome—to ignore the symptoms of Silent Sabotage. And here's why.

Few things in life have as much of an impact on people's lives as their jobs. It doesn't matter if you're the head of a giant corporation, or a messenger delivering packages through city streets, our jobs are barometers by which we measure our contributions to society and our own self-worth. When values break down in the workplace, the domino effect ripples straight through us and into every aspect of society. We feel abused and cheated. Our own sense of self-worth and value plummets. Divorce rates rise. Crime skyrockets. Alcoholism climbs. This, in turn, leads to a collapse in values in our neighborhoods. Eventually, values break down in government, they collapse in our criminal justice system, and slowly but surely they deteriorate throughout our cultural institutions. Much of this spreads silently until it is too late and Silent Sabotage spreads throughout our society like a cancer, destroying everything in sight.

Business is the last major institution to suffer the effects of eroding values. We're already infected and the disease is spreading. Nevertheless, business remains our best hope for correcting the problem. Why? The answer has a lot to do with our economic system. It forces people to work to survive, and that makes business—in one form or another—central to just about everybody.

So business is the only institution left that has the power to reach people at a grass roots level, and rebuild our shattered values system. Government can't mandate it. Organized religion hasn't made a convincing case for it. And our educational system isn't equipped to deal with it. Business, on the other hand, can make all the difference in the world.

Some might call this presumptuous—right in line with the same industry titans who once said, "What's right for General Motors is right for the country." That's not the case at all. Values transcend business. They are first and foremost about people. Because you and I depend so much on our jobs, and because what we do is such an integral part of who and what we are, business serves as the most logical arena from which to spearhead this effort.

I believe business is up to the task. Why? As I've noted before, it's becoming increasingly obvious that our current method of downsizing problems away isn't working. Restructuring does nothing for those who lose their jobs, and only creates greater anxiety for those who stay. It doesn't create better service, and it's certainly not doing much for productivity.

The second reason—business is beginning to realize that its own self-preservation depends on values. Values and business performance go hand in hand. Without one we can't have the other. So if you're asking yourself, "What is this all about?" and "are we doing the right thing?" don't be afraid of the answers. Business leaders are coming to the conclusion that shareholder wealth cannot be a basis for a company's existence. Moreover, people at every level of business are taking the right steps to address the situation. With each passing day, I'm seeing encouraging signs that business is on the right track—a track that will steer us away from Silent Sabotage and lead us all on a permanent path to rediscovering our values.

It can be done. Levi Strauss is making a fortune capitalizing on worldwide demand for jeans. Yet in 1992, the company surveyed its retailers and found them an unhappy lot. While the company made a great product, its ability to deliver on time was pretty poor. Levi chairman Robert Haas launched a full-scale effort to correct the situation. Out of that watershed effort, the company created values guidelines covering virtually every aspect of its business—from dealing with foreign contractors to environmental issues, individual behavior, diversity, communications, and safety and health requirements. Levi also audited more than 600 of its overseas contractors and severed ties with thirty of them because they failed to meet the new standards.

Haas, in a recent interview in *U.S. News & World Report,* said the company's new emphasis on values is turning out to be smart business on top of being the right thing to do. "Companies have to wake up to the fact that they are more than product on a shelf. They're better behavior as well."

Levi's values program is one of the most closely watched and scrutinized efforts around. *Business Week,* in an extensive cover story in its Aug. 1, 1994 issue, openly wondered whether the Levi approach was "visionary or flaky?" While the company got high marks for pursuing a values approach, some wonder whether employees are spending too much time on the effort at the expense of performance. To me, this just demonstrates the perils of short-term thinking. When you base your business on a values-based strategy, you're telling the world that you're in it for the long run. I'd be willing to bet that Levi's effort will pay off handsomely in the years to come.

At a recent meeting at a Ritz-Carlton Hotel, I happened to notice all the waiters and waitresses practicing their serving techniques prior to a big dinner. When was the last time you heard that happening? During the evening's dinner, the staff all served the bread in unison. Earlier in this book, we looked at Ritz-Carlton's service credo. It's a prime example of how to serve and create value. It's also paying off for the company. People notice the difference in the level of service and the way the organization and its people are perceived. Stories about the company's commitment to service appear regularly in major business publications and on network business shows.

The Levis and Ritz-Carltons of the world are still in the minority, but their ranks are growing everyday, and that's encouraging.

What's not so encouraging is the depth of the values crisis. For every Ritz-Carlton and Levi Strauss, there are at least 100 companies that have not yet addressed values. I ran across an alarming article recently in a newsletter put out by IndeCap Enterprises, which studies issues related to corporate restructuring and outsourcing.[1] The article states:

> A recent survey among CEOs of Michigan manufacturing companies . . . asked 'Do you consider your em-

[1] *Indecap Perspective*, August 1993, Vol. 2 Issue 4, p. 3.

ployees to be assets or liabilities to your company?'
Over 90% felt their employees were liabilities. We
haven't located more definitive survey sources to determine how generalizable these attitudes may be among
CEOs, but it represents a core of sentiment with inter-
esting restructuring implications ... the issue does
raise two very provocative questions that CEOs ought
to be addressing in their corporate restructuring programs:

1. Where are the people that really are assets to
the business?

2. What is being done to reduce the number of
liability employees?'"

This article speaks volumes about how far we still have
to go. Can you imagine what this portends for the future if the
heads of American corporations really perceive their employees as liabilities rather than assets? Many CEOs are so out of
touch with their employees, that in a way it's not such a surprising admission. But if this kind of attitude prevails, a lot of
companies are going to find out the hard way that you can
reorganize until you're blue in the face, you can downsize until there's just a handful of people left, but if they aren't treated
as *assets,* performance will never change. In fact, nothing positive will ever happen unless employees are treated as assets
and deeply respected as such.

As a proponent of shared values, I can tell you that this
examination and discovery process has made an enormous
difference in my life. As a business leader, I believe this process has, in fact, saved my company from disaster. As a concerned world citizen I believe shared values are not only right
for business, but right for the future of our society as a whole.

I must confess, however, that I am somewhat alarmed at the lack of urgency that values receive outside of the political campaign arena. It's time to get serious about it. It's time to take action, for we have very little time to make a difference. Shared values are the only way I know to stop Silent Sabotage.

If you are concerned about values in your own organizations, I urge you to trust your instincts. If you have cause to wonder, you probably have a cause that needs attention. I close by offering these insights:

- Values building is a process that needs everyone's support. It must be championed from the top of the organization, and it must take hold at a grass roots level.
- A shared values program isn't a "program of the month." It's a lifetime commitment. It will change the very scope of your organization. When it is done right, it will energize people like never before. If you are not prepared for such an outpouring, don't attempt it.
- Connect values with reasons. Providing a rationale for a value helps people remember it. It also helps them apply the logic of that value to new and different situations.
- Shared values requires openness. Everyone has to know as much about your business as possible. If your colleagues have questions about the business, how do you expect them to work together to transform shared values and common purposes into reality without total open honesty from all levels?
- Shared values requires consensus. Without buy-in, someone is left out in the cold. Building a shared values program will challenge your organization's interpersonal skills like never before. But it's worth it. When people say yes to one another, their relationship changes; a potential argu-

ment can become a reasoned dialogue. Diversity in the face of a challenge can become solidarity.

- Think of a values program as an internal compass that enables people to act responsibly and interdependently under a variety of conditions.

And finally, while I advocate urgency here, I also recommend a little patience. This may sound trite, but in this case it's true—old habits die hard. Creating a shared values program won't automatically change the way people act and think. But that doesn't mean we shouldn't try to break away from convention and old-line thinking. People are looking for change. In fact, sixty-seven percent of those surveyed by DBM recently thought that a "code of values" was very important to business. But only seven percent thought most companies lived by them.

Shared values are all about having faith and trust. If you are a business leader, have faith in your own people. It may take some time for them to see the light. But when they see a commitment to doing things differently—and when they see for themselves that this is truly a lifestyle change for the better—they will back this effort 100 percent. If you're not the head of your business or a senior level executive, don't give up. You can make a difference. You know the value of values. And you are on the leading edge of a movement that can have a profoundly beneficial effect on the future of your organization.

Sometimes it can be a lonely place. But you're going to have plenty of company soon.

Good luck.

Appendix
What is *Your* Trust Level?

Few issues strike more closely to the heart of values than *trust*. Without it, there is little room for common ground; no basis for developing an alignment between personal and organizational values. In a very real sense, trust is a cornerstone of the values foundation. Remove it and suddenly everything falls apart. By the same token, rebuilding values without an atmosphere of mutual trust risks everything. So it is essential that we examine our own trust levels by asking the following questions: How much—or how little—do we really trust our superiors, our subordinates, and our company? How much do the people we work for trust us? What about the individuals who work for us?

There is no easy way to assess levels of trust. We can't measure it in pounds or pints, we can't quantify it like a census, and it's hard to pinpoint feelings outside of extreme generalities. In one of my previous books, *Trust Me*, I concluded that a method of assessing trust would be a useful management tool. Together with Dr. Elaine Duffy, a psychologist, I've developed a series of surveys to measure trust levels among subordinates and managers. You've already seen one of these surveys in Chapter 7. Three more are included in this Appendix. Since virtually everyone assumes both roles in his or her business life, we suggest that you complete all four exercises. We've also found that these materials are most useful when both an individual's boss and subordinates complete them.

It's important to note that these surveys are not validated psychological instruments. They're learning tools that can help you and your boss or subordinate structure a dialogue about trusting relationships.

What will the results of these exercises show? A lot depends on how honest individual recipients are with themselves when answering the questions. If they are forthright and frank, the results should provide a clear assessment of where trust levels stand and how relationships should be improved. As an individual, your answers and scores can tell you a great deal about your attitudes regarding trust at your company. Combine and compare the results of all the individuals in a department—or an entire company—and you've gained a "big-picture" view of trust attitudes within the organization.

These results might be used, in turn, in the design of training programs, communication skills workshops, or performance appraisal systems, all focused on the goal of getting the very best possible from the company's principal resource: its people.

Trust Surveys: Who Do You Trust?

Each of the following surveys presents you with a series of descriptive statements.

If you *Strongly Agree* with the statement, write the number 4 in the box following it.

If you *Agree* with the statement, write the number 3.

If you *Disagree* with the statement write the number 2.

If you *Strongly Disagree* with the statement, write the number 1.

Once you've entered responses for all the statements in each survey, add up your total. The evaluations that follow each survey compare your score to that of people in positions similar to yours who have previously responded to the survey. Repeat this process for each survey.

Each survey has been developed as part of a larger project that involved hundreds of people from all management levels and from many different departments and types of organizations. Keep in mind, however, that they are only samples of longer questionnaires developed for use in large-scale projects. As such, they offer insight into general feelings, not exact measurements of trust levels.

Survey 1

Managers Trusting Subordinates

1. I make it a point to follow through on my promises. ☐

2. I delegate projects that enable my subordinates to attain success. ☐

3. I delegate as much work as possible without abdicating my own responsibilities. ☐

4. Each of my subordinates has the knowledge and skills required for his or her job. ☐

5. My subordinates believe that I have the knowledge and skills required for my job. ☐

6. My subordinates understand my style of management. ☐

7. My subordinates feel confident that the information I give them is accurate. ☐

8. My subordinates are aware that I take their opinions and suggestions seriously. ☐

9. I involve my subordinates in important decisions concerning the individual or the department. ☐

10. I can be relied on to handle work-related situations with good judgment. ☐

Total Score: _____

Evaluation: Survey 1
Managers Trusting Subordinates

If your score falls between:

10–20   Your Trust Quotient on this factor is low. You have real concerns about the quality of your communications with your subordinates, and you question the level of trust that exists in these relationships.

21–25   Your Trust Quotient on this factor is a little below average. You are concerned with your ability to trust your working relationships with some of your subordinates, and you may feel a need to improve your capability to work toward common goals.

26–34   Your Trust Quotient on this factor is somewhat above average. You feel that you have adequate working relationships with your subordinates, and you believe you can function well as a team.

35–40   Your Trust Quotient on this factor is at its highest level. You have a strong trust relationship with your subordinates, you feel that you communicate well with them, and you are confident that your team works together cohesively.

Survey 2

Subordinates Trusting Managers

1. My manager communicates that he or she respects my skills and abilities. ☐

2. My manager encourages me to take risks and make decisions. ☐

3. My manager always informs me about important matters that affect me. ☐

4. I feel free to tell my manager what's on my mind. ☐

5. My manager encourages me to develop and grow professionally. ☐

6. My manager has the skills and knowledge required for his or her job. ☐

7. My manager encourages me to determine my own objectives. ☐

8. I'm comfortable sharing personal thoughts or inner feelings with my manager. ☐

9. My efforts to demonstrate initiative are openly appreciated by my manager. ☐

10. My manager involves me in important decisions concerning me or my department. ☐

Total Score: _____

Evaluation: Survey 2
Subordinates Trusting Managers

If your score falls between:

10–20: Your Trust Quotient on this factor is at the lowest level. You feel your supervisor does not offer you much support, and you do not communicate openly and effectively with your manager.

20–25 Your Trust Quotient on this factor is a little below average. You would like to see some improvement in the level of trust that exists in your interaction with your boss, and you think that he or she needs to be more consistent in providing an environment of openness and support.

26–34 Your Trust Quotient on this factor is somewhat above average. You approve of the way you communicate with your boss, and you tend to feel comfortable with the general exchange of information and ideas between you and your manager.

35–40 Your Trust Quotient on this factor is at the highest level. You believe that you have an open and effective working relationship with your boss, and you believe that he or she has a real interest in your potential and your ideas.

Survey 3

Subordinates Trusting Top Management

1. The organization supports my manager's approach with his or her staff. ☐

2. My manager is loyal to me and to the department. ☐

3. I tend to be honest and truthful in my communications with my manager. ☐

4. Top management allocates resources to support innovation. ☐

5. The company supports my manager's performance appraisal policies. ☐

6. When necessary, I willingly submit to management's directives. ☐

7. My manager gives me frequent "pats on the back". ☐

8. The negative feedback I receive from my manager is helpful and constructive. ☐

9. My ideas and suggestions are heard by top management. ☐

10. My manager spends adequate time communicating with top management. ☐

Total Score: _____

Evaluation: Survey 3
Subordinates Trusting Top Management

If your score falls between:

10–20   Your Trust Quotient on this factor is at the lowest level. You feel isolated from top management and do not believe that your opinion and input are considered to be important. Your confidence in the directions of top management is questionable.

21–25   Your Trust Quotient on this factor is a little below average. You feel somewhat removed from top management and may be uncertain about the organization's ability to hear your ideas or those of your manager.

26–34   Your Trust Quotient on this factor is a little above average. You believe that there is an open line of communication with top management and that your skills and abilities, as well as those of your manager, are appreciated adequately.

35–40   Your Trust Quotient on this factor is at the highest level. You feel supported by top management and trust that you are recognized as a contributor to the organization.

Glossary of Terms

Alignment: When personal and organizational values are in synch, they are in a state of alignment.

Hierarchical: The layered, military-like organizational structures that still characterize many corporations today.

Micro-Manage: Refers to managers and organizations which over-manage by carefully monitoring or hovering over every detail of a project or task.

Mission Statement: A partnership between an organization and employees. Good mission statements tell what a company is all about. They state—clearly and succinctly—how everyone in the organization defines success. They also strike a balance between the company's goals, what it believes in, the people it serves, and the way it achieves success. It is a document that focuses primarily on the present.

Mores: Morals, customs, or beliefs.

Paradigm: An accepted model of doing business or performing a task.

Paternalistic: The nurturing, "we'll-take-care-of-you-for-life," attitude that characterized the relationship between companies and employees for decades in the United States and other developed nations.

Re-engineering: The redesign of work and critical business processes to achieve some radical improvement in business performance.

Shared Values: A process whereby organizations share their values in a way that encourages clients and suppliers to develop similar values programs of their own.

Silent Sabotage: A new phenomenon and a rarely examined social disease that is tearing apart the very fabric of society from within. Silent Sabotage is not one single problem, but the sum total of many problems converging at the same time. It's a turned-off, disenfranchised society that gives up in silent disapproval; it's a worker who comes in later and goes home earlier than he or she did ten years ago; it's a voter who never votes; it's people at work, at home, behind the wheel—anyplace at all—who just don't care about anything anymore.

Success: The qualities that lead an individual to feel as if he/she is making a contribution, is fulfilled and has achieved a sense of balance and inner peace, while achieving personal goals that are considered important. A critical component in determining values.

Values: What is considered important to a person or an organization.

Values/Ethics Code: A guideline of values that someone or an organization lives and operates by. Value codes brings values down to an everyday level, explaining in detail the qualities that the organization stands for and how to deal with real-life situations. Ideally, this should be a living document that changes with the organization and reflects the times. (Some organizations use this term interchangeably with Values Statement, Ethics Code, and Values Base.)

Values Crisis: A situation that exists when there is an imbalance in personal and organizational priorities; a basic lack of decency between people; a void in compassing and humanity.

Virtual Staff: A trend in today's workplace whereby a company will hire contract or agency workers to handle everyday tasks normally held by full-time employees. Virtual staffs often work on-site and in place of regular employees. Since they are not on the payroll, employers do not generally pay for benefits.

Vision Statement: A document that describes the future hopes and goals of the organization. It should capture the spirit of the organization while giving everyone connected with the business a sense of the adventure that lies ahead.

Index

AT&T values code, 115–17

Balance in one's life, 87–89
Bell & Howell, 71–72
Ben & Jerry's, 63
Boatmen's First National Bank, 125–26
Businesses
customer-oriented, 57
dependence on values, 150–51
with hierarchical structures, 52–56
paternalistic, 54–57
program based on values program, 120
role in rebuilding values system, 6, 150
values crisis in, 34
when employees are involved, 40
when employees don't care, 42–43
when leaders don't care, 39–41
when management and employees care, 48–49
See also Management; Organization

CBS, 72
Churchill, Winston, 9
Cin-Made, 46–47
Code of ethics. *See* Values code
Communications, 124

Complacency, 72, 74, 84
Consolidated Natural Gas mission statement, 107–11
Covey, Steven, 42
Crichton, Michael, 5–6
Customers
business base of, 58–59
customer-oriented businesses, 57–58
in functioning values program, 124
knowing, 64
response of hierarchical businesses to, 52–53
in values-based organization, 122

Walt Disney Enterprises, 65–66
Drake Beam Morin (DBM)
shared values program, 126–44
survey of trust and personal values, 12

Education, 32–34
Employees
appraisals based on values, 119
DBM contributions to shared values, 133–37
decision making role, 4
effect of exclusion, 41–42
in functioning values program, 124

Employees (*cont.*)
  mission statement role, 106–7
  obligation to employer, 64
  in paternalistic organizations, 55–56
  pre-DBM shared values program,
    127–28
  redefining success, 105–6
  shifting to new values, 47–48
  team approach, 59–60
  understanding perception of values
    and trust, 95–100
  as valuable resource, 60
  in value-based organization, 122
  virtual staffs as, 59
  vision statement role, 112–13
Environment
  DBM vision for organization's,
    130–32
  shifting to values-based, 44, 46–48
Ethics code
  as action plan, 24
  breakdown, 28–29
  corresponding values code, 20–21
  cultural orientation, 26
  of Drake Beam Morin, 62–63
  establishment of, 61–63
  outmoded, 56
  See also Values code
Ethics code, personal
  construction of a, 22
  for success as inner peace, 21–22

Faith, 31
Federal Express, 44
Flewelling, Ralph T., 25
Ford Motor Company, 66
Frey, Robert, 47

General Electric, 65, 103
Gerstner, Louis, 112
GM, 48–49

Haas, Robert, 147, 151
Hanna Anderson company, 63–64
Hierarchical organizations, 52–57,
  120–21
Honor code, 27–28

IBM, 72
Individualism, 57

Johnson & Johnson, 125

Keller, Helen, 1
Kirtman, Louis, 44–46
Korenblat, Ashley, 47

Lanto, Sandra, 133, 135–36
Levi Strauss, 44–45, 151–52
Locke, Edwin A., 112

Management
  as agent to change attitudes, 61
  creation of cooperative environ-
    ment, 46
  employee obligation to, 64
  resisting micro-management, 44
  role in organization rebuilding,
    43–44
  teambuilding, 60
  transition to team-based, 67
Managers
  gaining employee respect, 60
  with tunnel vision, 58
Merlin Metalworks, 47

Micro-management, 44
Mission statement
  developed by DBM employees,
    133–38
  developing, 106–11
  driven by ethics code, 61
  as tool, 114
Mores, sexual, 31–32
Motorola, 125

Organization
  defining success at level of, 82, 101
  individual perception of, 82–83
  purpose of, 86–87
  vision of, 111–14
  See also Businesses
Organization structure
  hierarchical, 52–57, 120–21
  implementing values program,
    123–24
  reflecting new commitment to
    values, 122–23

Paradigms, 129
Paternalism, 54–57
Patton, George S., 51
Peck, M. Scott, 16
Perception of organization, 82–83
Power base
  in functioning values program, 124
  in values-based organization,
    120–22
PSE&G electric business unit, 63

Reich, Robert, 39
Ritz-Carleton Hotel chain, 63, 152
Roosevelt, Theodore, v

Service
  in functioning values program, 124
  value of, 88–89
Shared values system
  case studies of rebuilt, 125–44
  commitment, 144
  DBM development and implementa-
    tion, 142–44
  developed by DBM employees,
    133–38
  examples of benefits, 125–27
  in implementation of values pro-
    gram, 119
  insights, 154–55
  steps in rebuilding, 92–124
  to stop *Silent Sabotage,* 154
Silent Sabotage
  components of, 43
  definition and manifestation, 4–5
  effect on values, 34
  overcoming effects of, 6
  signs of, 72–77
  upsurge, 31
Smith, Fred, 44, 45
Stradley, Carolyn, 45–46
Success
  in core of values crisis, 101
  defining, 82–86, 101–6
  employee perception of, 103–5
  exercises to understand attitudes
    about, 82, 85–88
  failed definitions, 101–3
  individual and organization percep-
    tions of, 88–89
  on individual level, 82, 84–85, 101
  as inner peace, 19–21
  at organizational level, 101–6

Success (*cont.*)
  organization perception of, 105
  questions related to, 85–86
  redefining, 105–6
Sun Tzu, 52
Surveys, 72–74

Team approach
  companies operating with, 65–67
  DBM Commitments Team, 138–42
  in mission statement development,
    107
  priority for, 66–67
  in redefining success, 105–6
Team-based management, 67
Townsend, Robert, 37
Toyota, 48–49, 55
Trust
  exercise to explore levels of, 97–
    100, 158–66
  importance in values system, 158
  new concept of, 59
  questions related to, 10–12
  restoration of, 93

Values
  business dependence on, 150–51
  current, 30–34
  defined, 12
  development of, 94–95
  erosion of, 31, 34
  evaluating company, 70–79
  individual, 129
  past, 27–30
  reengineering, 6, 67, 93–95, 144
  survey in reengineering process,
    72–74
  workplace breakdown, 148–50

Values, business
  alignment with personal values,
    93–94
  developing new, 74
Values, personal
  alignment with corporate values,
    93–94
  developing, 74
  evaluating, 17–18
  important, 12–13
  for inner peace, 22–24
  questions related to, 10–12
Values code
  assess perception of, 120
  of AT&T, 115–17
  common elements in, 117–18
  company-adopted, 34
  conditions for eroded, 13
  corresponding ethics code, 20–21
  development, 114–15
  rebuilding trust on new, 93
  trust based on, 93
  See also Ethics code
Values crisis
  in business, 34
  circumstances for, 14–15
  as illness, 16–17
  replaces Cold War crisis, 4
  success in core of, 101
Values system
  DBM Commitments Team, 138–
    42
  developing positive, 84
  development in DBM, 128
  effect of functioning, 123–24
  factors in erosion of, 78
  implementation of, 118–23
  purpose and vitality of, 121–23

signals of inadequate, 74–77
signs of erosion, 78–79
Virtual staffs, 59
Vision
  company, 111–12
  criteria for statement of, 112–14
  formation of company, 129–32

management setting of company's, 61
for organization, 44–45

Welch, Jack, 48, 65, 91, 103

Xerox, 72